VISIONARIES

See, believe, and live the life God has ordained for you.

Benjamin R. Aguirre

This book is dedicated to:

All of the Peters out there who feel alone and unloved. Those whose life could be better but isn't. This is for misfits, teenage moms, single parent children, and the broken in heart. This is for you, Peter's generation.

My wife Isela and son Austin
You are my inspiration and life. Thank you for your unending support and love. It's a privilege to be your husband, father, and best friend.

My parents

Thank you for your godly life, your words of wisdom, and your friendship. Your labor in the kingdom of God has impacted many lives, including mine.
The just man walketh in his integrity: his children are blessed after him (Proverbs 20:7).

To the visionary team (You know who you are)
Thanks for your words of encouragement and support that have helped me finish this book.

To the AJC youth ministry
You are the greatest youth group in the world! May God continue to unfold His plans for your life (Jeremiah 29:11).

CONTENTS

Chapter 1

THE CHALLENGE

Worse than being blind would be to be able to see
but not have any vision.
- Helen Keller

All day at school God had been urging me to talk to Him. My silent prayer in the bathroom stall no longer worked. Like a coke shaken up ready to explode, an intensifying desire to talk to God was building up within me and I could no longer hold it in. As soon as school finished, I quickly rushed home, dashed into my room, and fell on my knees in surrender to God's call to prayer. A few minutes into my prayer, I saw myself in a vision speaking to a congregation of young people. When I finished speaking, I began to lead a youth choir, in a song of worship. This was quite weird for me because some of the faces that I saw were young people from our local church. At that particular time we had no youth choir and the thought of our young people ministering was unheard of. Despite this, their facial expressions in my vision that day were different. They were so passionate and expressive in their worship as they were singing their song. I can't recall the song they were singing, but the response of the young people that they were ministering to was amazing. The Spirit of God moved like a great wave, crashing down upon all who were present in the sanctuary. The anointing of God was so thick it was almost tangible. Even though I wasn't physically there, I knew what I felt was God and He was speaking to me.

At this point my carnal mind began to rationalize and question, why us? I didn't fully understand why God would choose people such as us to minister in this magnitude. Then a verse came to me, *"But God has chosen the foolish things of the world to confound the wise; and God hath chosen the weak things of the world to confound the things which are mighty" (1 Corinthians 1:27).* I began to think, if a doctor healed the sick, people would credit the healing from the degrees that he held. If a singer went to the best music school and sang beautifully, people would give glory to the school he or she attended. But if someone does not come from the best singing school or does not have a Ph. D., then the only one that gets the glory is God. I then understood that God was raising up a group of ordinary young people to do something mighty for His glory. I immediately felt the weight of responsibility on me because the Lord had called me to bring this vision into reality.

At that moment, without any knowledge, I had just become a visionary.

God had shown me a glimpse of the future, but was I prepared for it? Was I ready for failure? Was I ready to leave my comfort zone? God told Abraham, *"Get thee out of thy country, and from thy kindred, and from thy father's house, unto a land that I will show thee" (Genesis 12:1-3).* What God was saying to Abraham was "I have a great work for you. I'm about to show you a land that I will give you and your descendents. You might not see it and you might not understand it all, Abraham, but you're going to pave the way. I will show you great things, but you need to leave your comfort zone."

That is exactly what God was challenging me to do that day. But, I too, had to leave my stagnant lifestyle in order for God to use me. In this hour God is looking for young men and women who are willing to dream big. Young people who are willing to leave their comfort zone of popularity, money, time, daily routine, and step out by faith to see the impossible. God is definitely looking for visionaries like Abraham in this last hour.

What is a visionary? A visionary is someone who can see beyond the tangible and find a way to bring the unseen into reality. God wants you to think and envision big things; things that are impossible for man, but possible for God. His Word says, *"...all things are possible to them that believe" (Mark 9:23).* So wake up and smell the aroma of the anointing that is upon you to do something great for God. The first and most important thing for you to do is believe.

NO VISION, NO PROGRESS

The reason why God wants you to be a visionary is so that you may have direction and know where you're going—going where, to the store? No, I'm talking about where you're going in life, in ministry, in a career. Don't we need to know where we are going in order to reach a destination? It's like getting into a car without knowing where to go. You'll be going around in circles all day and maybe even get lost. "What a waste of time," you say. Exactly! If you don't know where you're going, you're always going to be spinning your wheels in the same place and never getting to the place God has called you to go.

I am convinced that the biggest problem that young people face today is not peer pressure, not premarital sex, not even irresponsibility. It is...are you ready? A lack of vision! Yes, a lack of vision of where they're going and what their purpose is here on earth. Vision is so important because it doesn't focus on today; rather it focuses on tomorrow. If our focus is on our vision, we won't get side tracked by anyone or anything. This will result in our making progress toward our destination each day with the help of God. However, if we don't have vision we can either make terrible decisions that can alter our purpose in life, or we will end up spinning our wheels in the same place over and over again. Having no vision can lead to unwanted consequences of dissatisfaction, jealousy, bitterness, and frustration (just to name a few). Having no vision will block our growth, our knowledge, and our ability to attain goals. If we don't have vision, we certainly will perish in despair as the Word of God says, *"Where there is no vision, the people perish" (Proverbs 29:18).* God didn't create us and call us simply to do nothing productive for His glory. He didn't call us to live without accomplishing goals to advance His kingdom. He called us to have vision and follow through with it.

Why is there ongoing teenage pregnancy? Why do young people drop out of school? Once again, it is because they lack vision. If a girl saw herself ten years from now being a successful doctor who manages her own clinic, do you think she would want to mess her life up by making wrong decisions as a young person? I don't think so. If a young man saw himself ten years from now picking strawberries in a field and working as a security guard at night because he didn't have a high school diploma, do you think his views about dropping out of school would change?

If only people could catch a glimpse into what lies ahead of them. If only they would weigh the consequences that follow every decision, then they would make wiser choices. The problem is many young people don't have vision for tomorrow because it is hard for many of them to see the future as reality. A person without vision is like someone driving down the highway on a foggy day at 80 MPH. They can only see a few feet ahead of them, yet they continue to drive fast. They're liable of getting killed and harming someone else because their path, except for the few feet in front of them, is unclear and they don't know what really lies ahead of them. People that live without vision only see a few feet ahead of them; their today. Their path has been fogged up with disbelief and no direction. If you have vision, you will not be directionless. You will have a clear view of your today and your tomorrow.

I am talking about a personal vision that God wants to give you so you can see a glimpse of what lies ahead of you. Would you like to see your future? I bet you do. We all do. Who will I marry? Will I be successful? What will my ministry be? If you knew what was going to happen in the future, your whole perspective on life would change. I don't know your future, but God does. *Jeremiah 29:11* says, *"For I know the plans I have for you," declares the LORD, "Plans to prosper you and not to harm you, plans to give you hope and a future."* God wants us, His elect, to walk and live by faith and not by sight *(2 Corinthians 5:7)*. If your spiritual vision is blurred by other priorities like work, a "special friend," or anything that comes before the Lord, you only see what is before you at this moment in time - the tangible and temporal. You don't see the intangible, which is God's future for your life, His plan to prosper you and not hurt you. God wants you to live by faith. A visionary says I don't know how I'm going to get to the place God wants me to be, but by faith I'm going to hold on and let God do His thing.

Pastor Frank Damazio says, "Vision is that which a [person] perceives by the Holy Spirit as pertaining to God's purpose for them, thereby creating spiritual momentum resulting in spiritual advancement."[1]

Want to grow in God? Tired of having a meaningless life? Get vision. Vision enables us to see a glimpse of what God has in store for us, which in turn gives us meaning for our life right now. What? Yes, vision gives us energy to keep going while we are waiting for our purpose to be fulfilled. For instance, if I work at a crummy, lifeless job that pays me good, what keeps me at this job? What wakes me up every morning and drags me to work? It is simply the fact that every two weeks I know that I will be getting a good paycheck. The money is my motivation. Vision gives you the motivation to keep serving God because you know that in the end you will receive a crown of life.

WHAT DRIVES YOU?

Eastman Curtis told about a young man who was under his youth ministry that took no pride in personal hygiene. He said that this boy was "contaminated with bad breath and terrible body odor."[2] Curtis tried everything he could to convince this young man to keep himself clean and looking good but no matter what he was told, this young man never seemed to take his leader's advice. Then one day in a youth group gathering, Eastman Curtis noticed that this young man "was bathed, his hair and teeth were brushed, and he even had cologne on." What had happened was one day at school this young boy bumped into a "UFO (an unidentified female object)". Eastman says that the young man caught a vision of himself together with this young woman, and realized he would have to take better care of himself to make it happen. This vision provoked him to make an entire turn around in order to get what he wanted. Eastman Curtis says, "First comes vision. Then comes discipline."[3]

This filthy guy became a prince charming overnight. He already had the potential inside of him, but didn't have the drive to improve himself. Once again, the underlying problem of young people today isn't laziness or irresponsibility; it is the lack of vision. Once you get vision and do something about it, prepare yourself for a transformation.

Does a young man need to be forced to wake up at the crack of dawn to go work out? Not if he has the drive and purpose to get muscular. Each and every one of us has something that drives us to excel and do our best. Every morning there is a reason why you wake up, get dressed, and go to your destination. What drives you? What motivates you? As you answer these questions, you will find that what drives and motivates you is what your focus is. What drives and motivates you becomes your priority.

If a woman is what drives you then there is no problem spending a hundred dollars taking her to dinner, shopping, and having a great evening out. But when it comes time to give to God in offerings and tithes, do you complain and say that you have no money? If you're into skateboarding, you probably wake up every morning and skate three miles to school and ride in the skate park till evening. But do you make excuses that you can't go to church because you're tired and you don't have a ride, even though the church is only one mile away? What drives you?

King David was driven by God's presence. That drive woke him each morning and he said:

> *My voice shalt thou hear in the morning, O Lord; in the morning will I direct my prayer unto thee, and will look up.*
>
> *—Psalms 5:3*

His drive was to praise God:

> *I will praise you, O LORD, with all my heart; I will tell of all your wonders. I will be glad and rejoice in*

you; I will sing praise to your name, O Most High.
                                        —Psalms 9:1-2

His drive was to be available to God:

My heart says of you, "Seek his face!" Your face,
LORD, I will seek.
                                        —Psalms 27:8

His drive was to dwell in the house of the Lord:

One thing I ask of the LORD, this is what I seek: that
I may dwell in the house of the LORD all the days of
my life, to gaze upon the beauty of the LORD and to
seek him in his temple.
                                        —Psalms 27:4

We find that David did not complain about praying in the morn-ing, praising God, or being in the house of God for more than two hours on Sunday. His drive became his priority. In the good and in the bad times he said, *"I will bless the Lord at all times: His praise shall continually be in my mouth" (Psalms 34:1).*

If you have not gotten the main idea of this chapter by now, I'll tell you. You have no excuse not to live out your life the way God intended. Everything that you need in order to be used by God has already been stored within you from the time of your birth. You just need to activate it by stepping out in faith.

God wants to give you a *vision* that will *motivate* you into *action* so that you may live out your God given *purpose.*

Chapter 2

IT TAKES ONLY ONE

...Write the vision, and make it plain upon tables,
that he may run that readeth it. For the vision is yet
for an appointed time, but at the end it shall speak,
and not lie: though it tarry, wait for it; because it
will surely come, it will not tarry.

— *Habakkuk 2:2,3*

The vision that I received that day in prayer was the drive that shook and drove me out of my comfort zone. It reminded me of the call that was upon my life. Even though I didn't see it fulfilled right away, I believed God and began working toward this vision as the scripture above says *"though it tarry, wait for it; because it will surely come..."* Today God wants to speak to you and show you great things that pertain to your life and to your purpose. He wants to show you the big plans He has for you, and if you will be receptive and obey, your destiny will be changed forever as was mine. You must believe, act, and wait. The first thing I had to do was take God at His Word. *"God is not a man, that He should lie; neither the son of man, that He should repent: hath He said, and shall He not do it? Or hath He spoken, and shall He not make it good?" (Numbers 23:19).*

"...write the vision, and make it plain upon tables..."
Habakkuk 2:2

Next, I had to write down the promise that God had given me because it was something that I had never experienced before. I wanted to make sure that I wouldn't forget what God had told me. *If He said that He was going to use our youth group, then who was I to stop Him? Isn't He God? He can do anything,* I told myself. So I went to my pastor and asked him if I could start a youth choir. With his approval, I quickly spread the word to the youth group and musicians. As I gave the songs to the musicians, I envisioned a large youth choir singing at conferences and concerts. I thought of the many hearts that would be changed through their ministry. Writing down your vision will give you direction and it will serve as a reminder.

"...though it tarry, wait for it because it will surely come..."
Habakkuk 2:3

One thing I had to learn was that when God gives you a word or vision it doesn't mean that it will take place that day or the next. However, you can be sure that at God's appointed time it will come to pass as His Word says. When Abraham and Sarah received a word from God that they were going to have a child, it wasn't until twenty-five years later that the promise came to pass. Twenty-five years. Wow! Many of us become disappointed when God doesn't answer in two weeks. God's plans and purposes are for an appointed time. So wait and be patient. Your promise, Isaac, will come.

On the day of the first choir practice I arrived a half an hour early to pray. I was so excited because I had seen what God was going to do with our youth group. When the time for practice arrived, I lifted myself from prayer and looked up only to find that nobody was there. *What? How could this be*? In my vision, our youth choir had many people singing. Slowly, a few young people began making their way to the church for choir practice. To my disappointment, only nine showed up.

Because of our fast paced society and lifestyle, we often expect everything to be microwave-like. Just put your vision in and out comes a miracle! We expect our youth group and ministry to flourish overnight when we need to understand that God said, *"For my thoughts are not your thoughts, neither are your ways my ways, saith the Lord" (Isaiah 55:8).* God doesn't work around our timing, rather, He works around His timing and His timing is everything.

I began to exercise my faith and trusted that God's Word would come to pass. While in charge of the youth choir (more like a praise team) I grew spiritually in a way that my perspective on things changed. Things I used to do on weekends were no longer appealing to me, and the worship I gave God became more intense and more sincere. I was now involved with our youth group on a different level as God gave me strength and direction to lead them. At the same time I was developing a passionate devotional time with God. In my heart I always loved God and was always a leader, but I would use my strengths for temporal, unproductive things (getting my friends to ditch school-you get the point). I now started using my strengths for the glory of God - and it was easy to do. Soon my church friends joined the choir and we started to get more focused on godly things. We then began to witness to our friends at school who started coming to church. Many of whom were baptized; all because I believed God for His Word. If you stop using the strengths you put into temporal things and use them for spiritual things, get ready to see God work on your behalf!

JUST ONE VISIONARY

It only takes one visionary that can see beyond what your youth group is now and look at what they can become for the glory of God. Are you that one that can step out in faith and say, God, I give all my strengths and abilities over to you to do something great? It took me to see God's vision, answer to His call, and put my faith into action. This gave me the drive to share the vision and motivate others for a revolution. Had I not believed God for the vision, I would not have inspired others and we would have stayed in the same place. It takes only one to believe God for the vision and to transfer it to others.

What kept me going the first year with our nine to twelve young people was the vision. The vision of seeing young people minister to other young people at such a personal and powerful level, and myself being used by God to reach out to young people who were hurting inspired me to carry on. It gave me momentum to direct this choir of nine as though there were fifty. Because I stepped out, God confirmed the vision with his presence every time we sang.

There was a slow song we used to sing that would cause us to stop ministering because God's presence would just flood the sanctuary. I kept on believing God's word, *"For the vision is yet for an appointed time" (Habakkuk 2:3),* and the choir kept on growing as did my ministry.

As I conclude this chapter, I want to leave you with this verse. Read the words slowly and let the word of God speak to you.

> *That the God of our Lord Jesus Christ, the Father of glory, may give unto you the spirit of wisdom and revelation in the knowledge of him: the eyes of your understanding being enlightened; that ye may know what is the hope of his calling, and what the riches of the glory of his inheritance in the saints, and what is the exceeding greatness of his power to usward who believe, according to the working of his mighty power. (NIV)*
>
> *—Ephesians 1:17-19*

Chapter 3

DESTINY AWAITS

My family and I were in San Antonio, Texas for vacation and to our surprise, The Alamo Bowl was taking place that weekend. This annual event is much like the Rose Bowl in California where two college football teams play against each other for the trophy. People came from all over the United States to participate in this annual showdown. Several days before the event, people gathered around for rallies, while the college bands played up and down the River Walk. All of this was to build confidence and support in each team and momentum for the upcoming game. On the day of the event, fans painted themselves, wore their team's colors, and cheered ecstatically. The powerful energy was electrifying throughout the stadium as the fans and teams had one goal in mind. No matter what it was going to take, their main focus was on scoring the most points, which would lead them to victory. The purpose for all of these people coming to San Antonio was to be a part of the Alamo Bowl. The vision was to see their team win the trophy.

In our Christian walk this is where vision and purpose come hand in hand. You were placed on the Earth for a specific purpose, and vision is meant to give you direction to fulfill your purpose.

VISION GIVES YOU THE MOMENTUM TO LIVE OUT YOUR GOD-GIVEN PURPOSE

If there ever was a man who had a vision of where he was going, it was the Apostle Paul. He wrote:

> *I count myself to have apprehended: but this one thing I do, forgetting those things which are behind, and reaching forth unto those things which are before, I press toward the mark for the prize of the high calling of God in Christ Jesus.*
> —*Philippians 3:13-14*

While on his way to Damascus where he was going to persecute the Christians, God called the Apostle Paul. In Acts chapter 9 we find what Paul's purpose was: *"...he is a chosen vessel unto me, to bear my name before the Gentiles..." (Acts 9:15).* God revealed Himself to Paul and placed within him a great commission to be fulfilled, which was to minister to the gentiles. When God spoke, Paul immediately responded, *"Lord, what will thou have me to do?" (Acts 9:6).* When God speaks to you, you cannot help but to submit your will to Him.

There are many young people that God has been calling to do something great, but they hold off. They may be scared to make that commitment or not willing to let go of temporal things. Jesus once asked an individual to follow Him and to be His disciple, but the young man replied, *"Lord, suffer me first to go and bury my father" (Luke 9:59).* Jesus' response to this man's excuse was *"Let the dead bury their dead: but go thou and preach the kingdom of God" (Luke 9:60).* This young man wanted to serve God only at his time and convenience. Some young people today have the same attitude. They say, "When I'm done with college," or, "when I get a boy/girlfriend, I'll do what you ask of me." Is this the attitude God is looking for? Not so. God wants you to follow Him today and seek Him first. *"But seek ye first the kingdom of God, and his righteousness; and all these things shall be added unto you" (Matthew 6:33).*

WHAT ARE SOME EXCUSES THAT YOU HAVE BEEN GIVING GOD REGARDING THE CALL?

- **I'm too young. Look at Samuel (1 Samuel Ch. 3)**
- **I'm not smart enough. Look at Moses (Exodus Ch. 3 and 4)**
- **I'm a female. Look at Deborah (Judges Ch. 4)**

Whatever the excuse is, it's not good enough. God could care less what you have and what you don't have, or who you are, or who you are not; all He is looking for is availability. Could you imagine if Paul's response after the big encounter with God was, "Thanks for the offer, but not right now." What a loss it would have been to him and to all the people he ministered to had he not obeyed the call of God in his life. Yet, that is how many of you respond to God. He has been calling you and you've been putting Him aside. Even now, as you read this book, God is calling you to serve Him and love Him with all your heart, mind, and soul, today not tomorrow.

A LIFE IN RIGHT ORDER

I heard a story about a philosophy teacher who demonstrated to his class an illustration by using stones, pebbles, sand, and two empty containers. First, he placed large stones into one empty container. He then asked the class, "Will there also be room for all of these pebbles in the container?" Some of the students didn't think so. As the teacher carefully poured the pebbles into the container, he gave it a few shakes in order for the pebbles to work their way into the empty spaces between the rocks. He then showed them sand and asked them if the container would overflow if he added the sand as well. Most of them were sure that the container didn't have enough room to hold the sand. As he slowly poured the sand into the container and shook it lightly, the sand filled the empty spaces that the rocks and pebbles didn't fill up. Nothing overflowed because they were all in their right place and because they were put inside the jar in a specific order. The teacher then illustrated what would happen if he put the same components in the second jar only in the opposite order. After putting in the sand, the pebbles, and some stones, the jar overflowed because it couldn't contain all of the components. By doing this, he showed the class that the order of filling the container was necessary for everything to settle and fit in its place.

The large stones can represent your relationship with God, your relationship with your parents, and the community of believers in Christ, which is the church. The pebbles are the quality time you spend with your loved ones, perfecting your ministry, and your career. The grains of sand are the temporal things like dating, trying to find a mate, trying to look or be like someone else, and material things that really aren't important. The container represents you. What items have you placed first, second, and last in your life? Can you truly say that your life and priorities are in the right order? Are you caught up with the little things in life that take up the majority of your time and strength, causing the most important things to be pushed out of your life?

HOW IS YOUR VESSEL?

Is your vessel empty and clean, ready to be used by God? Or is it filled with temporal pleasures that take up all your time and energy, leaving your relationship with God, your talents, and gifts with little or no room to grow?

What takes up most of your time and strengths?
School   Boy/Girlfriend   Work   FriendsSports
Other: _____

List your top three priorities: _____

If God is not #1 on your list, then you need to reevaluate your priorities.

• *When making any decision, consider if it is in line with the great commandment:*

"...thou shalt love the Lord thy God with all thy <u>heart</u>, and with all thy <u>soul</u>, and with all thy <u>mind</u>." —Matthew 22:37

NOTHING CAN HOLD ME BACK

Paul understood that God had called him for a purpose and he had to stay focused. He had to forget his past reputation of martyring Stephen and many other Christians. He had to leave behind his criticizing friends and his childhood up-bringing and say, good-bye, I'm following Jesus. For all of the visionaries out there, you need to make up your mind to start living out your God given purpose. Even if you have to let go of some friends, quit that job that has been holding you down (you know the one that has you working on Sundays and during Youth Nights), and forget past failures. You need to *"look unto Jesus the author and finisher of our faith" (Hebrews 12:2)*. I had to get out of my comfort zone in order for God to use me. What do you have to put aside in order for God to use you?

Where do you see yourself five years from now? "I don't know", you say. You are one of the million directionless young people that don't know what to do with this precious life God has given you. That is why we have young people with undeclared majors and others who change their hair color weekly. It's because they can't make up their mind, they have no vision of where they're going, nor do they know how to productively invest their time. The Bible says that, *"A double minded man is unstable in all his ways" (James 1:8)*. This is why we must channel all of our strength, desire, and life to God so that He will make our life prosperous, otherwise we will be unstable. Paul understood that he was commissioned by God to do a great work. His mind was made up, and his goal was to see Jesus. *"To live is Christ, and to die is gain" (Philippians 1:21)*.

THE NEED FOR VISIONARIES

Why do we have scientists and doctors? So they can find the latest scientific breakthroughs and cures for diseases. Inventors are here so they can invent gadgets that will make our lives easier. Why visionaries? So there can be available young people that God can speak through to reach out to the lost in this last hour of the Church. God is calling you to make up your mind and live out your life the way He has ordained for you to live it. If you're not sold out for God and His purpose for you, then you will always live a life of uncertainty, wavering here and there. Could you imagine what would happen if the sun one day stopped shining and asked the moon, what's my purpose again? What if trees stopped producing fruit or electricity refused to produce power? What would happen if young people didn't live out their God-given purpose?

FOCUSING ON THE VISION

Sometimes our vision can be blurred with other things in life, but Paul knew that he had to reach for that high calling. Likewise, our ultimate goal as the children of God is to see Jesus one day. Until we get there, God has a vision for us, which is a glimpse of His purpose for us here on Earth. Once you get a vision and heed the call, it will be hard to get sidetracked with other things. The players at the Alamo Bowl, for example, had purposed within themselves to win the game. In order to win the game, they had to keep their eyes on the ball and not lose sight of their vision.

WHAT IS MY PURPOSE?

Why were you created? You were created for a reason. You were not a mistake. God has big plans for you, and He has placed a purpose in you that you must fulfill here on Earth. You may have been told numerous times that there is a reason that you are here, but you still wonder what that is. I wish I could tell you, but I can't. Just look at your strengths, personality, and character, including your surroundings; all of these are custom fit for your purpose. We have the misconception that ministry is just being a preacher or a singer and that's it, but there are endless gifts and ministries that God has placed in the hearts of His people to reach this world. Maybe you are a girl who loves to shop. You can use this for the kingdom of God by making it a ministry. You can buy clothes or nick-knacks, and put them in a special section of your church so when a new convert comes to Christ, you can offer them a special gift. Or if you're shy, you can send cards to encourage young people you haven't seen at church. If you are a "Hercules" kind of guy with muscles bulging out of your shirt (so you think), then you can flex those muscles and help out around the church. The Bible teaches us, *"...what ever you do, do all to the glory of*

God..." (1 Corinthians 10:31). In one of his seminars John Maxwell said, "Ministry is anything done in Jesus name." What you have (your strengths, talents, and personality) God placed in you for your purpose.

- *FIND YOUR STRENGTHS AND GIFTS*
  What do people complement you on? People never come up to me after church and say, "You sang awesome tonight!" Nor do they say, "You can really play those ivories." The reason why I don't hear them complement me in those areas is because neither singing nor playing an instrument is my gift. On the other hand, people complement me on preaching and leadership. Why? Because those are my strengths and gifts that God has given me. You will find that whatever your strengths are, people will complement you, confirming your gifts.

- *ASK GOD WHAT YOUR PURPOSE IS*
  The only person that knows the reason why a product was made is the creator or inventor of that product. Ask God why He created you. Why did Jesus Christ come here to Earth? To give us an example to live by and to die for our sins so we may have eternal life. Why was Moses put on this Earth? To help deliver Israel out of bondage and lead them toward the promise land. Why was Esther placed in the palace? To help deliver her people who were sentenced to death. Why do you live in the city you do, go to the school you attend, or congregate at your particular church? Seek God and He will show you.

*Meet Diane, **a young lady with a bad upbringing, but who was able to overcome and see the purpose God had for her.**
Hi my name is Diane. I have lived a hard life. I was taken from my parents because my dad was a drug addict and would beat my mom. I was separated from my parents and siblings and placed in a foster home. When I was twelve I was molested by my foster-father, and for years I harbored bitterness and hatred. At thirteen years old I didn't want to live anymore, but something never allowed me to take my life. I tried to find happiness by drinking alcohol, taking

drugs, and having sexual relations with older men who promised me a future but would always ultimately fail me. At one point I tried joining a cult in order to have some kind of identity and feel loved. As I tried to find myself I only ended up losing myself. When I was eighteen I was thrown out into the real world, which had nothing good to offer. Living on the streets and pleasing men was my life.

One day I met a girl on the bus whose appearance was different; her face glowed and her smile displayed real joy. She invited me to sit with her on the bus, and after a week we became friends. Then one day, she invited me to church. Having never gone to church, I was a little apprehensive but said yes. That evening while listening to the speaker, tears began to stream down my face. I looked around and saw young people who, I thought, probably had a good upbringing. I began to question God why I had to go through hell all my life. I asked Him, "If you are God, let me be like them." As the speaker was talking, he began to say words that I had never heard anyone say before. "If any man be in Christ he is a new creature." He continued, "The void you have in your heart cannot be filled by anyone. Only Jesus can fill it and complete you." The words began to minister to me, and I could feel God's presence all over me. This experience was something I'd never felt before. That evening, I gave my life completely over to God. As a result I've never been the same and the closer I get to God, the more He shows me my purpose. I now realize that there are other people that have had similar situations as my own who need to know about Jesus. It is my burden to share with them my testimony so that they too can give their life to Christ.

Diane could have become a victim of society. She could have blamed her biological father, foster-father, or ex-boyfriends and used them to make her comfortable in her misery. Instead she chose not to be a victim but a victor in Christ. Today as you read this book you may feel like what you have to offer God is not good enough. Your father may not be a minister, your mother may not be a singer, or your parents might not even go to church. You might even have a terrible, embarrassing past as did Diane. However, making excuses and looking at our shortcomings to justify what we're not doing for God is invalid because the Word of God says, *"Therefore if any man be in Christ, he is a new creature: old things are passed away;* *behold, all things are become new" (II Corinthians 5:17).* It's time that we become proactive in our decision making and not let circumstances dictate our future, our ministry, or our vision. We are not just ordinary people with flaws and weaknesses. We are the children of God.

Diane could have fallen back to the world; however, she had the mentality that Joseph had after his hardships. Even though he was betrayed by his brothers, sold into slavery, falsely accused, thrown into prison, and suffered other trials, his life's outcome was summed up in this sentence, *"But as for you, ye thought evil against me, but God meant it unto good, to bring to pass, as it is this day, to save much people alive" (Genesis 50:20).* Just as Joseph did, Diane was able to use all of her life's experiences as a testimony to reach out to others in the inner city and in her community, fulfilling her purpose. Her testimony is changing lives because there is power in a testimony.

> *"And they overcame him by the blood of the Lamb,* > *and by the word of their testimony..."* > *— Revelation 12:11*

God is calling you to a place where he wants to launch you out into ministry, yet some of you are still wondering, *"What do I have to offer God?* What can I possibly do for Him?" Remember the Sunday School lesson about the boy in the Bible who only had two fish and fives loaves of bread? The boy had enough food for himself, not for a humongous crowd. It definitely wasn't a lot of food, but it was enough for God to produce a miracle. With the little boy's food, 5,000 men alone were fed, not including women and children (Bible scholars say that there were approximately 20,000 people all together). After everyone had eaten, the disciples collected 12 baskets full of left over food. Just as the five loaves and two fish weren't much in the little boy's hands, a gift or strength may not be much in your own hands. However, when placed in the hands of the Master, your gift can be blessed, multiplied, and it can even change lives. God can use what you have to produce a miracle so that others may be blessed.

Because you are filled with purpose, God has given you the opportunity to reach out to people. Purpose is the intent or the reason why something or someone was made. You may not see the big picture of your purpose now, but God is calling out visionaries so He can show them a glimpse of what is in store for them.

Do you go to sleep and dream of being a mighty person for God? At church while the Spirit is moving, do you envision the sanctuary filled with thousands of people? These are visions, and if you can just hold on to them and remember them, they will help you in times of uncertainty. I could have given up on my walk with God a long time ago, but my vision always came back and reminded me how important I was. I knew that one wrong decision could ruin my life. Get the vision, fight for it, and hold on to it. It will come to pass at God's appointed time.

Chapter 4

DESTINY IS ALTERED

My wife and I assist in youth ministry at our church, and we try to challenge every young person to find his or her purpose and fulfill it. I find it funny when I hear young people say, "When I get married I'll be active in ministry and in the church. Praying and reading the Word of God will be much easier." The truth is you can't be anything you're not working on right now. You can't procrastinate until you get married and expect for your ministry to suddenly flourish after you've said, "I do." By the time you're married, you will have already developed bad habits, like procrastination and laziness, which will be of no benefit.

Singleness is one of the greatest seasons in life that God has given to mankind. It is a time to consecrate oneself to God, set priorities, and develop good habits. It is also a time that you are free. Free to be involved in your youth group, free to meet new friends, free to spend money on yourself, and free to give God what belongs to Him. The dangerous thing about having a free will is that God will not force His will on us. Because He allows us to make our own choices in life, we can alter His plans by choosing our own will over His.

UNEMPLOYED SAUL

God had great plans for King Saul, who He had anointed to be the first king in the monarchy of Israel. Because of King Saul's disobedience and impatience, everything was altered and the presence of God was no longer with him (*I Samuel* 13).

I hope that as you finish this chapter you will understand that God has a purpose for you and wants to do awesome things in your life. It's up to you, however, to follow through with God's will. Will you choose what God has planned for you, or will you make your own plans? Remember, if you get caught up in the temporal things of life, you can interfere in God's agenda and alter your destiny. It is never worth exchanging God's will for our own, as King Saul and others have learned.

ALL THE WRONG MOVES

Leo was the best looking guy at church and all the girls liked him. When he was seventeen, he had aspirations for ministry and a desire to follow the path of his father. The problem was that Leo never made his ministry a priority. Instead of praying and consecrating himself to God, he was out playing basketball, watching countless hours of television and on the phone with the girl of the week. In spite of his cold relationship with God, Leo would have visions of his ministry. He was going to be a preacher and maybe a pastor like his father. The times he was asked to speak God would use him mightily, and young people would confirm his calling by telling him how he ministered to their hearts. Nonetheless, Leo took it for granted and never committed wholeheartedly to God. "Next year, God," was Leo's response.

One day at school a girl began to flirt with him, and since none of the church kids were in his class, he flirted back. After a month of intense flirting, their relationship went a step further. Leo and his girlfriend would hang out after school and they would talk lustfully. Even though his heart wasn't in it, he continued to go to church and play the part. Leo's story is similar to that of some young people who act one way when they're in church and act different when they're out in the real world.

Because he was a senior in high school, Leo felt he was old enough to make decisions without informing his parents. He continued hanging out with his girlfriend and even took her to the prom.

One evening after graduation, she called him because her parents were out of town. The passion between them had intensified, and it could not be controlled any longer. The flirting no longer satisfied them. That night Leo went to her house and destiny was altered.

After all was said and done, Leo felt guilty about what had happened. He asked God to forgive him and shortly after, he broke off the relationship with his girlfriend. Leo knew he could not continue living the way he had been the past few months. Just when Leo was starting to move on with his life, he received a call he wasn't expecting. It was his ex-girlfriend, but he was determined not to stay on the phone with her for too long. To his surprise, he received some unexpected news, "I'm pregnant, Leo," she sobbed. Needless to say, Leo made his bed and had to sleep in it. Leo decided to marry this young girl when they were both at the peak of their youth. Their lives and destinies had been altered because of wrong choices they had made.

After several years of being a father and a husband, Leo never went back to church. He loved God but the memories of his past and his pride kept him away. One night while sleeping, he had a disturbing dream that seemed real. In this dream he saw a multitude of people in an auditorium worshipping and praising God. The worship and praise was tremendous and powerful, but it all came to an end when the people took their seats and waited to hear the Word of the Lord. Leo noticed that there was no one going to the pulpit. "What's going on? Who's going to preach to these people?" he asked. He saw the need and the hunger of the people, and then he saw confusion in their faces. At that moment in his dream, he heard God's voice say, "Leo, you were supposed to preach at this convention." Leo's heart began pounding uncontrollably. His breathing turned into panting, and his body was drenched with sweat. His mind went back...back to his teenage years when people would tell him how much he encouraged them through the Word of God. He was awestruck with disappointment and shame.

After a few moments, the scenery quickly changed. He saw a beautiful young woman sitting on a park bench crying. She was so distraught and consumed by her agony that she didn't care who saw her. Leo curiously bent down to see if there was anything he could do for this woman. "Ma'am, are you okay? Please, what can I do for you?" The lady didn't seem to notice that Leo was there. She couldn't hear or see him in front of her. Leo, moved with much compassion, desperately tried to help this woman, but she was not responding to him. Throughout the park he noticed mothers with their children, but this woman had no children around her. She was alone and in pain. Leo looked around, and then asked, "What's wrong with this woman? Why can't she hear me?"

Suddenly, Leo heard God say, "She is grieving because she is lonely. She has no husband or children. You were supposed to be her husband, Leo." Just then Leo took a closer look and realized that it was Sarah from his youth group. He remembered Sarah as being a God-fearing young lady. Leo had been interested in her, but she was too much of a "church-girl" for him at the time. Great pressure began to build on his chest. He couldn't handle the pain, the regret. *How could I have been so blind?* Leo thought. Tears began flowing down his face as great sobs of pain filled the air. Suddenly, he woke up and to his surprise his pillow and face were drenched in tears. *What a strange night,* he thought.

He tossed and turned in bed a few times in effort to find a good position, and soon he drifted off to sleep again. Leo had another dream. This time he saw a little girl on a hospital bed who was feeble and thin. She was also crying, Leo could no longer bear to see her in pain. The young girl reminded him of his daughter, and he was greatly moved. He asked God, "What's wrong with her?"

"She has leukemia," God replied.

Leo asked, "Where is the pastor? Why isn't he there to pray for her?"

God responded, "You were supposed to be the pastor, Leo. The responsibility was on you to pray for her. She will die soon." Leo nodded in disbelief. He couldn't take the pain and the guilt he felt. At that moment, he was awakened again and he fell on his knees by his bedside. Leo asked God to have mercy and to forgive him for his mistakes. He knew that this hadn't been an ordinary night and God was talking to him. Leo repented of his sins and told God he would serve Him again.

Leo is now attending his father's church…alone. His wife is of a different faith. And although she doesn't actively practice her faith, she refuses to let her daughter attend church with him. Had he chosen God's direction for his life, Leo would not be suffering like this. He shortchanged God's best for *his* best.

Like Leo, today many young people are playing with destiny, whether it's rushing down the aisle, or flirting with someone God hasn't intended for them. Soon they will have to pay the consequences for their decisions. The horrible truth is that once your destiny is altered, you can't go back in time and take back your mistakes. You will have to live and deal with your consequences for the rest of your life. Remember, you shouldn't live life without restraints (like Leo) because you are sure to run into trouble. You've been called and chosen by God so live a life of purity, of restraints and of godly wisdom.

I don't know if you realize this, but this generation needs you to carry out your God given purpose. What would have happened if Thomas Edison hadn't invented the light bulb? What if Martin Luther King Jr. hadn't stood up against segregation? What would have happened if Moses dwelt on the fact that his father and mother abandoned him as an infant by placing him in a basket and sending him down the river? What if he was stuck on the belief that his whole childhood was a lie and focused on the murder he committed? What if he had stayed in the wilderness? Who would've delivered Israel? Likewise, what would life be like if you choose not to follow God's plan?

EASILY REPLACEABLE

God's purpose for creating man and woman was that they might have dominion over the Earth, multiply and have a relationship with Him. Since Adam and Eve chose to make a wrong decision that altered God's ideal plan for mankind; we are all condemned to die. Everything was altered because of their temporary decision. I want to remind you of something I remind myself of often, and that is everyone, including myself, is replaceable. If we choose to do our own thing, God will raise up someone available who will do it. For example, Adam altered God's original plan for mankind (which was to have perfect communion with God), but God Himself easily replaced him. Jesus Christ came down and restored the relationship with mankind, took back the authority that was once Satan's, and passed it down to the church. No matter what your position, you can, and will be replaced, if you choose your own path.

In Leo's case, God had another speaker at that convention. Sarah did get married and had children of her own, and another pastor was placed in Leo's stead. God had all of these blessings planned for Leo to partake of, but unfortunately because he didn't have vision, he fell short of his purpose.

The urgency for young people to become visionaries is vital in this last hour because if they don't get a hold of vision, they may settle for temporal things that may drastically alter their destiny. Not only will you rob yourself of God's blessings if you choose to live without vision, but you will also rob others of their blessing. How? Your ministry and purpose is meant to further God's kingdom and touch lives. If you fail in this area, you are missing out on God's best for your life, and the people who could benefit from your ministry will miss out as well. However, keep in mind that God is sure to raise someone else that is willing to carry out what He desires if you choose to disregard His call.

SCRIPTURES TO MEDITATE ON:

Before I formed you in the womb I knew you, before you were born I set you apart.
—Jeremiah 1:5

Yet I still belong to you; you are holding my right hand. You will keep on guiding me with your counsel, leading me to a glorious destiny.
—Psalm 73:23-24, (NLT)

Chapter 5

GROW UP!

+≈≈+

Wanted: Spiritual Toddlers
POD (Prince of Darkness) seeks PIB (Permanently Immature
Believers) to serve as underground servants for his kingdom.
Must know very few verses by heart, pray only when in trouble,
consider happiness a main goal, are bickering, jealous, and
quarrelsome, infrequently attend church, rarely tithe, rarely
study Scripture, and above all must not share the gospel with
others. [4]

If anyone would like to rob you of your vision and purpose, it's
Satan because he knows you were created to mess up his plans.
Since he understands the power that resides in you to turn his world
upside down, there is nothing more threatening to him than young
people filled with purpose. Young people who are willing to do
something great for God, and who have a vision on how to get
there. Young people that are *"confident of this very thing, that He
which hath begun a good work in you will perform it until the day of
Jesus Christ" (Philippians 1:6).* Visionaries are those who know
they were born with a purpose, and until that purpose is fulfilled
they are untouchable. They know Satan can't touch them because
they are ambassadors of Christ, and they have countless angel
bodyguards who protect them daily. God has placed purpose, gifts,

and talents in your life and will provide the means necessary for you to carry out His work.

As a visionary, I was ready to do great things for God, but God had to first put me in Joseph's school of brokenness. When you are a visionary there will be great oppositions in your life that will either make you or break you. They will either make you better or bitter.

We can learn a lot from Joseph, a chosen vessel whom God gave dreams to and the wisdom to interpret them. He realized that the Lord had called him at a young age for a special purpose. In Joseph, we can see many similarities that mirror us. His father gave him a coat of many colors; our Heavenly Father robes us with His righteousness. Joseph had dreams; the Bible says," ... *young men shall see visions..." (Joel 2:28).* Joseph was despised by his brothers; Jesus said that we would be persecuted for His name sake.

Visionaries will always face opposition from Satan, relatives, church members, and co-workers. The hard thing about being a visionary is that only you have seen a glimpse of what God has in store for you, not everyone else. It is best not to share what God has revealed to you to just anyone because not everyone will believe it nor will they support you. On the contrary, some people will mock you and despise you just as Joseph's brothers mocked him. Genesis 37:8 says, *"...And they hated him yet the more for his dreams, and for his words."* Remember when Noah warned the people about the vision of rain that God had given him? I bet they mocked him in disbelief. Unbelievers mocked Jesus Christ Himself all the time. So remember, if you share your revelation with just anyone, be prepared for opposition.

When we started the youth choir, the people I thought would support us, did not. Instead of encouraging us, I believe they said in their hearts, *We give them six months. Then they'll die off.* It was very difficult at first to work for God with opposition, and when I began to preach it got worse. I was criticized because I didn't say the right words, I would stutter and say "um" a thousand times. I wanted to give up. Ever since I stepped out to preach and lead the young people it seemed like my life got worse. Negative things started happening within my family; my parents were having health problems, my past didn't seem to go away and bad thoughts started bombarding my mind. It was a warpath! Yet as I endured all the arrows from the enemy I found myself getting closer to God, and I witnessed many lives that were changed through His power. The final outcome proved to be worth it all.

The same was true for Joseph. As fast as the dreams came to him was as fast as he was stripped and thrown in a pit. Are you in a pit right now? You might have just come back from youth camp or finished a youth revival, and you saw great things in the future for your ministry. Maybe the preacher gave you a word from God, and you came back hyped to do God's will only to find out: your parents are divorcing, your boyfriend is breaking up with you, crazy thoughts are flooding your mind, your having sexual feelings, you feel like your going to lose your mind! Don't get discouraged; there is a process. Satan knows that greatness resides in you, so he is working overtime to destroy that which has been birthed within.

The Bible is full of stories with people who were called by God, and whom Satan tried to destroy. Satan tried to destroy Daniel by putting him in the Lion's den; Shadrach, Meshach, and Abednego, by putting them in the fiery furnace; Jesus, by killing young infants at the time of His birth and attempting to kill Him all of His life on Earth until the crucifixion. But Satan's plan didn't work because *"greater is he that is in me than he that is in the world" (1 John 4:4).* Satan can try to destroy us, but the Bible says, *"No weapon that is formed against thee shall prosper..." (Isaiah 57:14).*

A preacher once said that Paul describes Satan like a roaring lion because that is all he can do. Lion's that roar all the time are those that are old and have no teeth. They will roar to intimidate other animals because if the others find out that they have no teeth, they will be easily defeated. That's the way Satan is. He can only roar at you to bring fear in your life, but he cannot touch you. When you believe and recognize that Satan has no power over you and that you have the Lion of Judah on your side, you can overcome anything. *"God has not given us the spirit of fear; but of power, love and a sound mind" (2 Timothy 1:7).*

It is of great importance that young people today get a hold of God's living Word because we need it to sustain us during hard times. I think it would be quite strange for a young man at the age of nineteen to still be in diapers and drinking from a bottle. Wouldn't you? Well, there are many young people that are still drinking a bottle when God wants to feed them the meat of the Word for growth and maturation. A prerequisite in becoming a visionary is to grow up!

WE ARE EITHER DRAWING CLOSER TO GOD OR MOVING FURTHER AWAY FROM HIM.

> *Brethren, I count not myself to have apprehended: but this one thing I do, forgetting those things which are behind, and reaching forth unto those things which are before, I press toward the mark for the prize of the high calling of God in Christ Jesus.*
> —*Philippians 3:13-14*

Everyday we should experience a new encounter with God. Our Christian walk should not be lived from Sunday-to-Sunday. It should be dependent on a daily relationship with God Himself. What scares me about revival is that a lot of times it doesn't take much effort to produce an atmosphere of worship, praise and power at church. Because church is happenin' we feel that we no longer need to pray or read the Word of God as much. Since the church is in revival, new people are coming through the doors, and young people are on fire, we feel like we can put our relationship with God on "cruise control." By doing this, do you think we're getting closer or further away from God? In order to see our purpose fulfilled we need to be *"instant in season and out of season" (2 Timothy 4:2)*.

"I write to you, little children, because your sins are forgiven..." (1 John 2:12). Notice that John was making reference to the spiritual "little children" who he was reminding about the fundamentals of salvation. Still, many of us, as young people, are fixated on this first passage of scripture and that's it. We have experienced God's grace, been washed by His powerful blood, and that's all we know of God; we've never grown any bigger. Every Sunday we say, "I love you Jesus," but God says, "Are you following my commandments?" Even nature itself shows us that life is all about growing up. When

you plant a seed, it grows and matures, bearing fruit or a flower. When a child is born, you can't stop him or her from growing physically and developing mentally because it's part of nature. We also need to grow up spiritually. It is our responsibility to be strong in the Word of God and overcome the enemy. We can't depend on our pastor or youth pastor to feed us a word from God while we sit back and do nothing. If we expect to grow spiritually, we need to search the scriptures and speak to God.

God's will is for us to move from the milk of the Word of God to the meat of the Word. When He has a T-bone steak to give us, He wants us to chew, swallow, and break it down further in our stomach. He wants us to explore His Word and meditate on it so that we may grow. He isn't just our Savior who forgave our sins; that's what we know of Him in the baby stage. He is also our provider, He is our strong tower, He is our Everlasting Father, He is our Supplier, our Healer, and our Righteous Judge. God wants us to grow up so we can be like *"A tree planted by the rivers of water that bringeth forth fruit..." (Psalm 1:3).*

Joseph was a young man who was raised in the faith of his forefathers. He had developed a relationship with God that kept him going even through his trying process. He believed every word his parents told him about the God of his grandfather, Isaac, and great-grandfather, Abraham. He remembered how God promised Abraham that He would make him a great nation, and how his great grandmother Sarah gave birth at an old age to Isaac. Joseph and his forefathers show us that there is a big difference between being religious and believing God's Word. Joseph didn't have the Bible like we do, but his faith was so great that he believed the great writings and testimonies of times past. First we see Joseph as a gifted vessel of God, and later we find this visionary stripped, betrayed, and in a pit. Just when things couldn't get any worse, he goes from the pit to slavery. What kept Joseph going, despite all of this turmoil, were his dreams and his faith in God. How much do you believe the spoken word of God?

In *Luke 9:57* we find a certain man that came to Jesus and wanted to follow Him. Jesus' response was, *"The foxes have holes, and the birds of the air have nests, but the Son of man hath nowhere to lay his head" (Luke 9:58).* Today there are many young people like this man who want to serve Jesus because of the powerful things He has done. Jesus was saying, it's more than what you see right now, for soon I will be betrayed and will walk a lonely road to Calvary and be crucified. Likewise, some young people commit to serving God as long as everything is going their way. What would happen if their parents were to get divorced? How would they respond if young people started leaving their church to go to a bigger church? What would they do when their friends betray them? Would their commitment to God be the same as it was when everything was going fine? Would they throw in the towel, become bitter, and hang out with bad company?

ARE YOU A CARROT, EGG, OR A COFFEE BEAN?

A daughter complained to her father about her life and how things were so hard for her. She did not know how she was going to make it and wanted to give up. She was tired of fighting and struggling. It seemed as one problem was solved a new one arose.

Her father, a chef, took her to the kitchen. He filled three pots with water and placed each one on a high fire. Soon the pots came to a boil. In one he placed carrots, in the second he placed eggs, and the last he placed ground coffee beans. He let them sit and boil, without saying a word.

The daughter sucked her teeth and impatiently waited, wondering what he was doing. In about twenty minutes he went and turned off the burners. He fished the carrots out and placed them in a bowl. He pulled the eggs out and placed them in a bowl. Then he ladled the coffee out and placed them it in a bowl. Turning to her he asked. "Darling, what do you see?"

"Carrots, eggs, and coffee," she replied.

He brought her closer and asked her to feel the carrots. She did and noted that they were soft. He then asked her to take an egg and break it. After pulling off the shell, she observed the hard-boiled egg. Finally, he asked her to sip the coffee. She smiled as she tasted its rich aroma.

She humbly asked "What does it mean father?"

He explained that each of them had faced the same adversity, boiling water, but each reacted differently.

The carrot went in strong, hard, and unrelenting. But after being subjected to the boiling water, it softened and became weak.

The egg had been fragile. Its thin outer shell had protected its liquid interior. But after sitting through the boiling water, its inside became hardened.

The ground coffee beans were unique however. After they were in the boiling water, they had changed the water.[5]

DO CIRCUMSTANCES CHANGE YOUR LIFE OR DO YOU CHANGE CIRCUMSTANCES?

How do you respond toward fiery trials? If you are founded on the Word of God, come what may, you will be able to stand still and say, *"I am more than a conqueror" (Romans 8:37).* How is your attitude toward the trials in your life? Don't you know that after you have been tried through the fire you will come out as pure gold? The key to surviving trials is how you perceive them. Even when things get unbearable, throw yourself a party in spite of your circumstances.

HOW TO THROW YOURSELF A PARTY

1. Think of the great things that God is going to do in your life through this circumstance.
2. Read a chapter of Psalms.
3. Confess that you serve a great God.
4. Listen to inspiring music to encourage your soul.
5. Attend church service regularly.

If any one had an excuse to be bitter and to be a victim, it was Joseph. After being thrown into the pit, Potipher, a very well established individual in Egypt, bought Joseph as a slave. Because Joseph was his father's favorite, he had not had to do much work (must be nice). As a slave, all of a sudden he now had to scrub the grime off floors and work like never before. I can just imagine all of the frustration and bitterness he must have felt, but he never turned his back on God.

Like Diane in the previous chapter, God can use any predicament or situation that you may have gone through for a particular purpose. You might have been sexually or physically abused, maybe your dad cheated on your mom or maybe you grew up poor. Regardless of your situation, God can use it for your purpose, which is to win the lost. I am blessed to have been raised in church and to have both of my parents in my life. I really can't relate to young people who have done drugs or who come from a divorced home. However, an individual whom God delivered and preserved from a bad upbringing can minister to a person with a similar situation. God can use your life experiences to further the gospel.

If Joseph hadn't gone through what he did, his family and thousands of people would have starved to death due to a famine *(Genesis 41 - 42)*. He went through all of this in order to see his dreams fulfilled. Joseph was put in the right place at the right time even though it cost him tears, brokenness, and many years from his family. In the process of your vision unfolding there will be opposition. These oppositions, however, are needed to strengthen you for ministry. If you are willing to be a visionary and want to make a difference in your community, what are you willing to go through?

RUN, JOSEPH, RUN

Joseph was a good-looking and hard working young man who probably carried a lot of inner frustrations about life. It was during this time of brokenness that an opportunity arose where Joseph could have given in to pressure. He could have said, "God I give up, I don't need these trials." It was the well-known incident with Potipher's wife that was going to make him or break him. Potipher's wife tempted Joseph. She tried to seduce him when no one was looking *(Genesis 39:7-13)*. *The moment is right*, Joseph could have thought. *Maybe all my worries and frustrations will go away.* But Joseph loved his God more than any woman, and didn't give into temptation. He didn't want to mess up the dream God had given him, so he chose not give in to his master's wife. This resulted in false accusation and Joseph was sent to prison. Now how about that? Joseph got in trouble after doing the right thing.

How would you have responded?

Young men, you may be laughed at and called a mamma's boy if you don't sleep with a young lady. You may even be called boring because you don't party and drink beer like everyone else. What they don't realize is that you don't want your dream to die and that you value life and God more than anything that is temporal.

BABIES LACK DISCERNMENT

Previously we discussed the importance of growing up by reading God's Word, and how not reading the Bible will result in staying in the nursery. Warren Wiersbe believes that babies lack one thing and that is discernment.[6] If you do not have God's Word in your heart, you will be easily deceived by anything that comes your way. The Bible encourages us *"That we henceforth be no more children, tossed to and fro, and carried about with every wind of doctrine, by the sleight of men, and cunning craftiness, whereby they lie in wait to deceive" (Ephesians 4:14).*

Many young people fall in sin over and over again. Do you ever wonder why? It is because they haven't grown up. If Satan can keep them in the nursery, he will be content because he knows they will fall for anything. Notice how there are young people who sway with the trends of this world. One day they dress like they're in a gang and another day they dress like preppies. They are unstable because the Word of God is not in them. Even some of the young people in our church pews are captive of sin every day of the week because they have probably given in to pornography on the web, lustful desires and listening to music that endorses sexuality, violence, and drug use. As a consequence, every Sunday for an hour and a half these young people sit in our church pews, condemned of their sins. Instead of praising God, they're asking Him for forgiveness because they haven't grown up.

God is calling young people out of the nursery and into the church to minister *"for such a time as this" (Esther 4:14).* God does not want you to experience His mercies and stay in the outer court all the time. He desires to meet with you in the Holy of Holies. If you want to be a visionary then you need to grow up.

"… I have written unto you, young men, because ye are strong, and the word of God abideth in you, and ye have overcome the wicked one" (1 John 2:14).

Notice the scripture says that these young men are strong, the Word of God dwells in them, and they have overcome the wicked one. In order to overcome temptation and trials, we must have the Word of God in us. When we have His Word engrafted in our hearts, we will be strong. Without the Word in our lives we will not be able to overcome the wiles of the devil. We will be swayed to and fro and be defeated on a daily basis. God's desire is for us to overcome sin, not for sin to overcome us. If the Word dwells in us, we will *"overcome the wicked one" (I John 2:14).*

Overcoming is doing as Joseph did. He had an opportunity to sin with Potipher's wife, but refused to give in. That is an over-comer.

Visionaries are so full of the Word of God that no matter what comes their way, they understand that they have a purpose and nothing is going to stop them-not even temptation. If you want to be like Joseph, an overcomer, you need to be strong in the knowledge of scripture.

KEY TO BEING AN OVERCOMER

God told Joshua that the key to success was to read and meditate on His Word:

> *This book of the law shall not depart from your mouth, but you shall meditate in it day and night, that you may observe to do according to all that is written in it. For then you will make your way prosperous, and then you will have good success.*
> *— Joshua 1:8*

David also found the key to be an over-comer:

> *Your word I have hidden in my heart, that I might not sin against you.*
> *—Psalms 119:11*

TO ALL VISIONARIES

If you want your youth group to grow up, get them in the Word of God. Dancing, shouting, and music is all good, but it's even better when mixed in with the Word of God. Read it and fall in love with it. It has romance, suspense, violence, and drama. Once you begin reading it, you will not be able to put it down. It is *"a lamp unto our feet and our light unto our path" (Psalms 119:105).*

Get into the Word of God! You will still be faced with sin and temptation, but you will also have sound doctrine to resist its enticements, and overcome them.

> *For the weapons of our warfare are not carnal but mighty in God for pulling down strongholds...*
> —*II Corinthians 10:4.*

HERE ARE SOME STEPS TO GET STARTED:

1. Find a study Bible that you are able to understand
*The NIV or Message Bibles have conversational English, which may be easier to read instead of the "thee's", and "thou's".

Some I recommend:
Thomson Chain Study Bible
1 Minute Bible- Doug Fields

2. Attend bible studies consistently
3. Memorize scripture
- Find a partner and write several scriptures on a 3 x 5 card and take turns going over the verse.
- Read a verse slowly repeating it over and over again

4. Pray for wisdom

MISSION: COMPLETE
Joseph's dreams finally came true. He was united with his family and they fell at his feet, just as he had envisioned in his dreams. Everything that he went through was to be revealed at that moment. Joseph had been placed in a high office in which he was able to save his family from the famine.

Hang in there I know it's hard and you might have many

unanswered questions, but just believe that God is going to use you through these hard situations. While you're waiting for your purpose to come into fulfillment grow in the Word of God. When you're focused on His Word, God will show you great and mighty things. All you need to do is grow up!

Chapter 6

THE GRASSHOPPER VERSUS
THE VISIONARY

+≈+

For as he thinketh in his heart, so is he...
Proverbs 23:7

During their spring break, five young people went on a road trip to Yellowstone National Park. At first everyone was excited, but after many hours of traveling, three of the five began to get antsy and troublesome. They started complaining about how long the trip was taking. Soon, their negativity influenced the rest of the young people in the car, so they made a u-turn and headed for home. What they didn't realize was they were already in the park and only several minutes away from the welcome sign.

In Numbers, chapter thirteen, we find one of the saddest incidents in the Bible. The children of Israel were only eleven days from the land that God had promised Abraham and his descendants, but they wouldn't see it for another forty years *(Deuteronomy 1:8)*. God told Moses to send men, one from each tribe, to spy out their land of promise and bring back a report. *"Send thou men, that they may search the land of Canaan, which I give unto the children of Israel..." (Numbers 13:2)*.

When the spies returned to inform Moses and the people, all but two gave a bad report.

*And they brought up an evil report of the land which
they had searched unto the children of Israel saying,
The land, through which we have gone to search it, is
a land that eateth up the inhabitants thereof; and all
the people that we saw in it are men of a great stature.
And there we saw the giants, the sons of Anak, which
come of the giants; and we were in our own sight as
grasshoppers, and so we were in their sight.*
—Numbers 13:32

Negative people seem to always give a bad report. It's amazing
how their interpretation of a situation is always negative. I know
there are none at your church, but at the church I attend, there is
always a negative person who tries to bring opposition to the vision.
I do not like fellowshipping with negative people because they
disturb my spirit. They bring heaviness to every project and every
gathering. They complain, gossip, and try to poison every person
that comes their way.

When God gave me the vision of what He was going to do for
our youth group, not all of the young people were supportive.
Nonetheless, there were nine that had the same mindset, and that
was all God needed. God doesn't need all of your young people; He
needs at least one that can believe Him for the impossible.

The men who went to spy out the land had a negative spirit to
begin with. They saw the glass half empty and not half full. Since
their perception was already poisoned with negativity, they gave a
bad report, and consequently, it spread like wild fire. Negative
people have the power to destroy the faith in others by bringing
doubt, fear, discouragement, and dissension.

The children of Israel witnessed God's mighty acts. They lived
through the plagues that afflicted Egypt. They saw the power of
God move upon the Red Sea and how He divided the waters so they
could walk on dry ground. Their provider supplied them with
"wonder bread," which rained from heaven. This great God, who
was a pillar of cloud by day and of fire by night, did all of these
miraculous things for them. Yet, these people who witnessed the
wonders of God let several cold, no-prayer-life, negative spies

convince them that they were as grasshoppers; and guess what? They believed it!

God has great things that He wants to do for you and your youth group. You are at the brink of a great revival for your soul and for your community, but God wants you to evaluate your friends and your thinking. If they are negative, that will hinder you from seeing your promise.

The children of Israel were only eleven days from entering the promise land, but because of the negative attitudes of certain individuals, their "conquering giants" mentality became that of a grasshopper's. If you want to be a visionary, you can't allow negativity in your life because it will destroy your future and ministry. It will rob you from God's promises for your life.

GRASSHOPPER 411

Let me tell you a little bit about grasshoppers. First of all, Grasshoppers hatch only in the spring and summer, when the temperature is warm. They refuse to hatch during cold seasons. In church, grasshoppers come out when there is revival and the Spirit of God is moving and convicting hearts. They hatch when the fire of the Holy Ghost begins warming things up. During revivals, churches split, marriages fall apart, and Christians decide to turn their back on God. Why? Because Satan knows there is power when God's people unite, so he uses any tactic possible to attack the church.

Second, grasshoppers do not migrate. Once a grasshopper finds territorial land, it will not leave until its death. They do not like going anywhere beside the places they know. There are some Christians who refuse to grow in God and who refuse to go to unknown places in the spirit. These grasshoppers will hinder you from growing in God. They will tell you that your vision and purpose for your life is impossible. Like the spies who only knew Egypt and refused to go further toward their promise land, people with a grasshopper mentality will hinder your advancement in the things of God. The negative spies doubted God's Word. They were conformed to their ways, so their attitudes influenced countless people to stay in the wilderness.

If you are going to be a visionary, you need to always be ready to go to new places in the spirit. The Bible says that we are to go from glory to glory. God didn't intend for us to stay in the same place all of our lives nor did He intend for us to stay in the same place for several months. Everyday is a new day, a new challenge, and another opportunity to fulfill your mission here on Earth. You cannot fall into complacency because time is too short. There is a lot of work to be done.

It is important that you evaluate your progress often. Where are you today in God? What or whom is keeping you from living a fulfilled life? If you have the mentality of a grasshopper, five years from now you will find yourself in the same bench, doing the same thing, bitter about everyone because you are in the same rut you are in, while everyone around you is successful in ministry.

Another interesting fact about grasshoppers is they can lay up to 200 eggs at one time! It takes only a few grasshoppers to multiply into thousands because they can reproduce rapidly. It took only eleven men to transfer a negative perception into thousands of people, which resulted in thousands of negative people. It only takes one person to spoil and destroy your youth group.

After the spies gave their evil report and after the people were poisoned, they *"murmured against Moses and against Aaron: and the whole congregation said unto them, would God that we had died in the land of Egypt!" (Numbers 14:2).* They also wanted to make for themselves a new captain and return to Egypt. Joshua and Caleb, who were among the spies, tried to convince the people that the land was theirs, but because the people had already been poisoned, the Israelites refused to accept a good report.

> *And they spake unto all the company of the children of Israel, saying, The land, which we passed through to search it, is an exceeding good land. If the Lord delight in us, then he will bring us into this land, and give it us; a land which floweth with milk and honey. Only rebel not ye against the Lord, neither fear ye the people of the land; for they are bread for us: their defense is departed from them, and the Lord is with us: fear them not. But all the congregation bade*

stone them with stones..."

—Numbers 14:7-10

People with no vision will easily believe an evil report, which will cause negativity to spread quickly. Once negativity has spread, it is difficult to bring out the good, as we learned with the children of Israel. *"But it takes only one wrong person among you to infect all the others- a little yeast spreads quickly through the batch of dough" (Galatians 5:9).*

Another fact about grasshoppers is they will eat every thing in sight. Grasshoppers eat 25% of available forage in the Western US. That is what will happen if your youth group has the mentality of grasshoppers. They will eat every good thing that comes their way. If you hang out with negative friends you will find yourself trying to destroy someone that is faithfully serving God. You soon will notice yourself talking about your pastor and his family, and all the young people in your youth group. You will get bitter when someone gets better. You know you have a grasshopper mentality when you destroy instead of build.

GOD CAN'T BE BIGGER THAN YOUR PROBLEMS UNTIL HE BECOMES BIGGER THROUGH YOUR PERCEPTION

I believe the one thing that angered God was the fact that the children of Israel made the Canaanites bigger than Him. They doubted God's power by believing the bad report of the negative grasshopper spies. The promise land was filled with blessings in abundance, but it also had giants that intimidated them. You have a promise from God, but will you allow someone with a negative perception to intimidate you and cause you to doubt Him? If the obstacles seem to be bigger than your promise, then you are perceiving the obstacles bigger than God. *How big is your God?*

If you are wondering how big your God is, take a look at Job. Job, the man that woke up one day and lost everything including his children, was left confounded and silent after asking God to explain why he had to go through his dilemma. God replied:

Who is this that questions my wisdom with such ignorant words? Brace yourself, because I have some questions for you, and you must answer them. Where were you when I laid the foundations of the earth? Tell me, if you know so much. Do you know how its dimensions were determined and who did the surveying? What supports its foundations, and who laid its cornerstone as the morning stars sang together and all the angels shouted for joy?
—Job 38:1-7

Today God is calling you out of your comfort zone and telling you that He has a great work for you. Who are you to tell him, "But my parents don't go to church," " I failed you before," "What do I have to offer?" Watch out because He will leave you silent like Job, blind like Paul or with a limp like Jacob. You need to respond by faith and believe God will do His part.

The children of Israel depended on the bad news they heard and doubted God. Because of their grasshopper mentality, they wandered in the wilderness for forty years. Many of our churches are in the state that they are in because of the mentality they have. *We are just a little church across the railroad tracks.* These churches say and believe they can't have revival like the church down the street. Sometimes many people believe that God can't use them like He is using other young men or women who have stepped out by faith. The fact is that God wants to use you and your church, but you need to change your thinking about Him and His work.

WE WALK BY FAITH, NOT BY SIGHT —2 Corinthians. 5:7

We need to start talking and walking by faith. Isn't that what visionaries do? What is faith? Let's take a look at two different definitions of faith. Prentice Mulford said, "Faith is power to believe and power to see..."[7] The Bible says, *"Now faith is the substance of things hoped for, the evidence of things not seen" (Hebrews 11:1)*

The only way you will grow in faith is if you grow in your relationship with God. When you have a devotional life, not only will you draw closer to God, you will start to believe His promises because your eyes of understanding will be opened. So it is very vital that you have a relationship with God. Then you will be able to trust in God until the promise comes to pass.

WE WILL BECOME WHAT WE SAY AND BELIEVE WE ARE

- Your youth group is second because you say it is.
- You will be a failure because you say you are.
- You're ugly because you think you are.

There is no rest in your mind or assurance for your future with that kind of thinking. You are speaking a curse to yourself and cannot please God with this kind of mentality. This is carnal thinking. You are supposed to think on: "...*whatsoever things are true, ...honest, ...just, ...pure, ...lovely, ...of good report; if there be any virtue and if there be any praise, think on these things" (Philippians 4:8).*

The reason you need to focus on the above things is because, *"For to be carnally minded is death; but to be spiritually minded is life and peace. Because the carnal mind is enmity against God ...so then they that are in the flesh cannot please God" (Romans 8:3-7).*

If you want to be a visionary and an overcomer like we discussed in our previous chapter, you need to understand who you are in God and how important it is to develop your spiritual life because through the Word of God you will find your identity in Christ.

> *...for as many are led by the Spirit of God, they are the <u>sons </u>of God (Romans 8:14).*

> *And if children, then <u>heirs</u> of God... (Romans 8:17).*

> *And we know that all things work together for the good of them that love God, to them that are called according to his purpose (Romans 8:28).*

Young people who are always struggling with the things of God, those that always want to throw in the towel, have a shallow perception because their relationship with God is weak. Our mentality as believers should be: little problems, big God. Could you imagine if our youth groups had the mentality that God can do wonders? God would break open a revival in the midst of those that are hungry for His presence.

The spies had seen the promise land, but didn't have faith to claim it. Instead they influenced others with their wrong mentality, causing everyone to miss out on God's promise. Likewise, those young people so close to Yellowstone National Park were influenced by negative remarks, and they missed out on what could have been a great time. It is really important that you know who your friends are, because they can hinder you from reaching your promise.

WHAT FRUITS ARE YOU KNOWN FOR?

- Dissension or discord
- Gossip
- Defiant to authority
- Jealousy

The Bible says, *"Either make the tree sound, and its fruit sound, or make the tree rotten, and it's fruit rotten; for the tree is known and recognized and judged by its fruit"* (Matthew 12:33).

EVALUATE YOUR FRIENDS

It is important to remember that your friends can either rob you from your promise or help you.

a. Do your friends have a prayer life?
$\qquad$ Yes $\qquad$ No

b. How many times in a conversation do your friends gossip about the pastor and his family, the brethren, and the young people
1 2 3 4 5

c. Do they encourage you to do things for God?
$\qquad$ Yes $\qquad$ No

d. Where do they see themselves five years from now?

_____

_____

In order for us as visionaries to see the promise, we need to feed our mind with three things :

1. Prayer

> *Not by might nor by power but by my spirit saith the Lord...*
> —*Zechariah 4:6*

Notice, when you do not talk to an individual for a while, you have nothing in common. You can hear a pin drop during your conversation. This is how it is when we don't talk to God. We lose the connection with Him and learn to rely on our feelings and emotions, which will keep us in the wilderness.

2. Faith

> *For verily I say unto you, that whosoever shall say unto this mountain, Be thou removed, and be thou cast into the sea; and shall not doubt in your heart, but shall believe that those things which he saith shall come to pass; he shall have whatsoever he saith.*
> —*Mark 11:23*

If God spoke a word in your life, then by faith believe that it shall come to pass, because His Word shall not return unto Him void. His word is forever established in heaven and because He is God, you need to stand on His Word and believe it. At His time, your promise will come.

3. Assurance

> *And we know that all things work together for good to them that love God, to them who are called according to his purpose.*
>
> *—Romans 8:28*

When you get into a plane, you trust the pilot to take you to your destination. Visionaries have an assurance that God is going to take them to higher places. Come what may, they have the assurance that *"all things work together for good to them that love God...and called according to his purpose" (Romans 8:28).*

This generation will miss this awesome opportunity of end-time revival if our mentality is that of grasshoppers.

Chapter 7

AND GOD MADE ME LAUGH

*Is anything too hard for the Lord? At the time appointed I will
return unto thee, according to the time of life, and shall have a son.*
Genesis 18:14

He hath made everything beautiful in His time.
Ecclesiastes 3:11

One evening at our mid-week Youth Life Lesson, my good
friend, Kim, was admonishing our young people not to give up
praying. She said, "It may seem like you have been praying the same
prayer for weeks, months and years, and there is no answer." She
encouraged our young people by reminding them about women in
the Bible, like Hannah and Elizabeth, who cried out to God in prayer
because they were barren. Kim described the pain they must have
felt to see friends and family members give birth, while their womb
was barren. Year after year, they expectantly waited for an answer to
their prayer, yet their womb remained closed. After many years of
prayer and supplication, they witnessed the answer to their prayers.

Kim spoke about King David, who as a young shepherd boy,
was anointed by Samuel to be king. We can only imagine how he
must have felt that day, but it wasn't his time to take the throne.

Instead, David would spend most of his youth running for his life from King Saul. Nevertheless, David held on to the promise God had given him. He continued to pray, praise and believe that the promise would come to pass. At God's appointed time, David became king of Israel.

Kim continued to speak as an oracle of God, "God is saying, 'Keep on praying for the mother who is not saved, the father who does drugs, and the cousin who is sick with cancer. But know that your thoughts are not like mine. You may want an answer tonight or tomorrow, but my ways are so much higher and better than yours. I will answer them according to my timing.'" Young people fell on their faces and cried out to God in response. Just then, the Spirit of God spoke to me and said, "Tell my young people to leave Hagar's tent."

You see, God promised Abraham and Sarah a son, but she wouldn't give birth to that promise for twenty-five years *(Genesis 15:4-5)*. Because her biological clock was ticking and because she didn't see God's promise unfold according to her timing, she relied on her own plans instead. Therefore, Sarah took matters into her own hands and told Abraham to go into her handmaiden, Hagar, to produce the promise.

It is important to understand that God doesn't work around our timing. He works according to His plan for our lives because He is *"the author and finisher of our faith" (Hebrews 12:2)*. He knows the beginning, middle and end of our book because He is the writer. Those who get impatient with God and choose to do things their way take authorship of their book. Unfortunately, these people alter or miss out on God's plan for their life and have to pay the consequences for their mistakes, as Sarah and Abraham had to.

Today, do you trust God? Are you convinced that God is in control with your life? Are you allowing God to author your book, or are you in Hagar's tent working out your own plans? Sarah thought her way of bringing forth the promise was good because she was not seeing any results; she was not getting pregnant. There are many young people who try to do God a favor by making decisions on their own because they don't see God's promises fulfilled right away. I want to let you know it doesn't work that way. If we want God's will to be fulfilled in our life, then we must let Him do the writing of our book. We must not interfere by making our own plans. When you seek God's will for your life, you need not just have faith, but you also need to trust Him.

Proverbs 3:5 says, *"Trust in the Lord with all thine heart; and lean not unto thine own understanding."* Yet, many young people seem to do the opposite of this scripture and instead make their own: *Trust in yourself and your feelings, and lean on your own understanding.*

This was Sarah's concept. No longer did she trust in what God had in store for her and Abraham. Now she was leaning on *her* feelings and *her* understanding. Feelings are deceiving because they are temporary and unstable. For instance, when a young man and woman have strong sexual feelings, they are but for a moment. If they choose to give in to these feelings, when the moment of passion is over, they will have to face the consequences of guilt and shame. Notice how opposite these feelings are. At one point, they were at an ultimate peek of ecstasy, and at another, they were at a low state of disappointment. Our feelings are unreliable. The Word of God says, *"The heart is deceitful above all things, and desperately wicked: who can know it?" (Jeremiah 17:9).*

This is why, in order to live a victorious life, you need the ingredients that we have been talking about:

1. A relationship with God
2. Knowing the Word of God
3. Faith
4. Trust in God

If you do not believe God is big enough to work on your behalf, regardless of the situation, then one of the ingredients above is missing in your life.

God has a purpose for everything and knows the appointed time to bring forth His will. Earlier, we read about a barren woman, by the name of Hannah, who continually pleaded to God for a child. At God's time, she gave birth to Samuel, a prophet and judge, who ruled over Israel and guided them in the things of God. What would have happened if Samuel were born earlier or later? He would not have been as useful as he was at the intended time in which he was born.

Elizabeth was also persistent in prayer and asked God to bless her with a child. At the Lord's appointed time, He caused her to become impregnated with a powerful man of God, John the Baptist, who paved the way for the Messiah.

There is a reason why you're not married yet. There is a reason why your parents haven't come to God yet. There is also a reason why your purpose hasn't fully been revealed to you. Don't be discouraged. While you wait, just learn to trust and grow in Him!

When it comes to relationships, I truly believe God has someone special in mind for you to marry someday - in His time. He/she might be across the country or could be sitting on the other side of your church. During your time of singleness, however, God has given you the opportunity to build and prepare yourself for your future mate. God knows your faults and weaknesses and loves you so much that He is willing to work on you before marriage so no major issues will cripple your relationship. Instead, both you and your mate will be able to help each other grow in the things of God.

MEET LINDA

Linda was a young lady who was passionate about God. She was active in the youth group and loved to sing in the youth choir. At 16 years of age, she began to feel distraught as she allowed negative thoughts to cloud her mind. She felt like an old maid because she never had a boyfriend. For a majority of Linda's years as a young person, she never seemed to excel in the things of God because she was too busy trying to find herself a mate. At 18, she met a guy who was fairly new to the church, and Linda fell in love with him.

Soon they began courting and six months into the relationship, Linda and Martin decided to get married. The pastor, along with the youth pastor, opposed the decision because Martin was fairly new and they didn't know much about his background. They both told her she had great ministry potential and could be hindered if she rushed into marriage. The pastor warned her that if she persisted, something would happen to this marriage because it was not in God's perfect will. In spite of this, Linda did not heed to council and married Martin. Months in the marriage, Martin left the church.

Soon thereafter, he began to drink and party with his friends. What Linda did not know prior to their marriage was that Martin had never healed from his childhood. He experienced brutal abuse from his father who would strip and beat him and his mother. As a result, Martin was full of resentment and hatred. Consequently, he fell into the same mold of his abusive father. Martin wanted to heal, but marriage demanded too much of him so he gave up and went back to drinking.

Linda was now involved in an abusive marriage where her drunken husband would tie her up to the headboard, rape, beat and humiliate her. After a beating that almost left her dead, Linda knew that if she didn't leave, it would cost her life. Linda divorced Martin and continued to serve God on her own.

Just as Linda tried to speed up God's timing, Sarah was anxious to speed up God's promises and told Abraham to go into Hagar's tent. We can relate Sarah, Abraham, and Hagar with our own life. Abraham represents time, your body, ministry, career, and goals; God gives us a promise for the future. Sarah represents us; when the promise hasn't been fulfilled we seek to take matters into our own hands. Hagar is the visible solution to your promise; instead of waiting, we go after what we can see or what we think God wants for us.

Maybe you feel that your time clock is ticking because you're twenty-two and not married yet. Perhaps you've said, "I'll help God chose the right mate for me since He hasn't answered my prayer. Forget ministry. I'll settle for a good paying job." Many people are easily lured by their sight and feelings and not by faith. They are like the children of Israel who were close to receiving their promise, yet because their physical sight influenced them, they missed out on the unseen promise.

If you make decisions that are not according to God's Word, then you will have to pay the consequences later in life; you reap what you sow. You didn't have to ask Abraham twice to please the flesh. There he went into Hagar's tent. Likewise, your feelings can lure you into making decisions that you feel are right and if you are carnally minded then you will do whatever your feelings tell you to do.

Many times, we convince ourselves that there is a better solution to our current situation. Rather than trusting God for what He has promised us, we resort to our carnal reasoning and end up doing something God didn't intend for us to do, as did Sarah and Abraham. Sarah's feelings told Abraham to go into Hagar's tent. Since Hagar came from Egypt, she represents the world. When we rely on our carnal thinking, we exchange our promises with the world. God is trying to tell us, "Why settle for worldly affairs when I have all of heaven to bless you with?"

Hagar conceived and gave birth to Ishmael. He was Abraham's son, but not the son of promise. *Genesis 17:18-19* says:

> *And Abraham said to God, Oh that Ishmael might live before thee! And God said, Sarah thy wife shall bear thee a son indeed; and thou shalt call his name Isaac: and I will establish my covenant with him for an everlasting covenant, and with his seed after him.*

Many times we make decisions for our lives that are not in the perfect will of God, and we expect God to bless the mess we got ourselves into. When Hagar conceived, she despised Sarah. When Isaac came into the picture, Ishmael scoffed him, provoking Sarah to throw both Hagar and Ishmael out of their home. Understand that disobedience is not rewarding. After you have gambled your chances and disobeyed God, your sin will come back to mock and despise you.

As visionaries, sometimes people find themselves trying to rush God's plan for their life. For example, some who feel called to preach desire for the pastor to automatically give them a spot on Sunday. Some who feel God has called them into music ministry want to play like a professional overnight. Whatever your desire and calling may be, remember that it will unfold in God's time. Meanwhile, know that God is taking you through a learning process that is of much value because it is building your character. Throughout the Bible, we find men and women of God who went through a learning process, a process of brokenness that changed their lives and prepared them to carry out their God-given tasks.

If Linda would have waited on God and obeyed her pastor and youth pastor, she would not have suffered as she did. Because she chose not to wait, her disobedience gave birth to an Ishmael, which wasn't the promise. Although we don't know exactly what Linda's promise could have been, we know that it would have been a rewarding one. Unfortunately for Linda, now Ishmael has turned around to despise and mock her.

While you're waiting for your Isaac (promise), meditate on these scriptures:

> *For I know the thoughts that I think toward you, saith the Lord, thoughts of peace, and not of evil, to give you and expected end (Jeremiah 29:11).*

> *To everything there is a season, and a time to every purpose under heaven (Ecclesiastes 3:1).*

Consider the choices that you are making right now. Are they forcing your promises into the world's tent, or are you keeping your promises close to your heart? The following is a self-evaluation that should help you recognize if you're placing your promises in the enemy's tent or in the temple of the Holy Ghost:

- Are you always trying to find your lifetime mate?
- Do you get depressed or discouraged if you're not in a relationship?
- Do you pray to God about your interest in the opposite sex?
- Is your boy/girlfriend serving God with their whole heart?
- Are you and your boy/girlfriend in a sexual relationship?
- Do you put God first in everything you do?
- Does your job interfere with church activities?
- Does your job provide an atmosphere for you to fall into sin?
- Does your new car or other expenses drain your finances, preventing you from tithing?
- Is the career you are choosing going to be a blessing or a hindrance to your ministry and your service to God?

AND THEY LIVED HAPPILY EVER AFTER?

- A young lady named Natasha was in love. After years of trying to find happiness with a man, she thought she finally found the "right" guy. All was wonderful until the day Natasha told her man she was pregnant. Now, Tom constantly reminds her that he doesn't love her and the only reason he is with her is because she got pregnant.
- James, a paralytic, is a prisoner in his own body. Although he once led a normal life, everything was drastically altered in one night. After his parents warned him not to go with his friends to a party, James refused to obey. In spite of barely coming back to church, James couldn't resist going out with his friends for the last time. On their way home, they collided with another vehicle. All of the passengers, except James and a friend, died. James was paralyzed from the neck down, while his friend suffered severe brain damage.
- Suzette lives an uncomfortable life because at seventeen she decided to sneak out one evening with the most popular boy on the football team. She gave in to having sex with him after being convinced that this jock really loved her. Not knowing that she was one of many sexual partners that he had, Suzette was later diagnosed with herpes. Now she has found the man of her dreams that loves her with all his heart, but how is she going to tell him that she has herpes? Will he stay or will he leave?

Do you think God wants your life story to finish like the ones just mentioned? Definitely not. That is why you need to trust God with your life and believe that His way is better than your way.

- A young career woman was ready to settle down and get married. After falling in love with the man of her dreams, life was at its best. On a romantic evening out, he proposed and they were off making wedding plans. A few months later, she noticed he wasn't returning her phone calls, and he had stopped visiting her. Her fiancé disappeared from her life. At first the pain was unbearable. It seemed like somebody had ripped her heart out. Many times she wondered what she was going to do. She began to resent God because He allowed this to happen. Several months later, she received unexpected news. Her former fiancé had AIDS. When she heard this, she fell on her knees and asked God to forgive her for being angry. She realized He had protected her from death.

Any time we take our trust off of God and make decisions on our own, we will find our plans and dreams in shambles once it is all said and done. If you notice in the examples given in this chapter, the people had no idea that their way was going to end in regret and shame. Today, people who make their own plans don't see the consequences that sin will bring tomorrow. This is why we need spiritual vision.

Vision is important because it allows you to see the future even though you can't literally see it. Vision gives you hope. Abraham and Sarah couldn't see Isaac but as they grew in faith, they believed that he was going to come. Not at their time but at God's time. Today Sarah is telling you to learn from her mistakes. She is telling you not to lean on your own understanding but to trust in God in all things.

The Bible says that Sarah named her son Isaac, which means God brings laughter. When your purpose is fulfilled, it will bring you laughter because you will realize that God truly had your life in His hands. He will leave you dumbfounded, amazed, and awestruck after his plan is fulfilled in your life. Sarah sums up her story with God by saying, "And God made me laugh." We hope this is the ending of your story - that God made you laugh, that there's joy in your ministry, in your marriage, in your career, and in your family.

Chapter 8

PETER'S GENERATION

In a high school class, sat a junior by the name of Peter. Peter was an odd ball compared to the other students. He had adopted a new, frightful appearance that was easily recognizable; black clothing invaded his wardrobe and somehow, he managed to get countless piercings on his body. He was kind of scary looking, which caused people to stay further away from him, and he wasn't easy to get along with. But that was merely the outer appearance of Peter.

Let me tell you about the real Peter that no one knew about. When Peter was eight years old, his mom left the house never to return again. His father was a drug user and an alcoholic who always had parties at his apartment and allowed countless strangers into his home. He didn't seem to have second thoughts about putting his son in an unsafe and dangerous environment. As a child, Peter's surroundings never seemed to affect him. He had become an independent child who would wake up each morning on his own. He then had to dress and feed himself, if there was any food at all. After school, Peter would come home hoping that there was something in the cupboard or fridge to snack on. Successful or not, he would attempt to prepare his own dinner, while his father and his fathers friends slept the whole day with hangovers.

The frustration started to build when he entered junior high, and people noticed that he wore the same raggedy clothes that didn't smell too pleasant. As his peers started making fun of him, bitterness and resentment began to stir up inside. Peter soon woke up to the harsh reality that he didn't have a mother, and his father was a druggie. Ignorantly, he blamed it all on himself. He believed that had he never been born, his parents wouldn't have split up. Years of carrying the blame, along with no one to talk to, resulted in a wounded heart; Peter soon died within.

One night in his bathroom, he thought about three students who were in his history class and who attended church across the street from his apartment. Peter's curiosity grew, and he wondered what it would be like to go to church. *Can someone really feel God?* He thought. *Is there really a God who cares about me?* Questions continued to flood his mind, but since his three church classmates didn't seem to have an answer, doubt settled in his heart all the more.

The girl who sat in front of Peter never told him about God because she was too heart broken about her split with her boyfriend. Everyday she would cry and be depressed about the breakup, while Peter thought, *If she could only experience what I am going through.* The boy to his right was always concerned about sports, video games, and the latest movies. He didn't care much about anything else but those three things. Peter said to himself, *I wish he would ask me to play basketball with him.* He also remembered the other young man across the room and how much he hated him, not only because of his big ego, but also because his conversation was always about sex and how many girls he slept with. For a while Peter didn't see this guy going to church, but every Sunday morning Peter's curiosity provoked him to wonder if God was real.

He would look out the window and would see these three young people step out of their car with their families, smiling as they walked inside church. Peter told himself, *Church must not be good enough to go to, because if it were, then one of them would have told me about their church and God.* As he reflected on these individuals, who could have been his hope to a brighter day, he was convinced that life was a misfortune. Since these young people never took time to tell Peter about the living God, he found no reason to live. So that night in the bathroom, Peter lay in a puddle of blood - He had taken his life.

Peter finally got to go inside that church he was always curious about, but this time it was for his funeral. No longer did he have to worry about his looks or if they would accept him if he walked through those doors; the casket was closed. Peter's three classmates attended the funeral. He would now see the God he was so curious about, but only for a short time because his final destiny was far from heaven above. I wonder how many Peters, in our school, our workplace, and our neighborhood, we pass up each day that have a story to tell. Who will listen to them? Who will tell them about Christ?

> *Go therefore and make disciples of all nations...*
> *(Matthew 28:19)*

God is raising visionaries to reach Peter's generation. If there is ever a time for young people to heed to the call it is now. Who will go?

> *I looked for a man among them who would build up*
> *the wall and stand before me in the gap on behalf of*
> *the land so I would not destroy it, but I found none*
> *(Ezekiel 22:30).*

Will you be like the three young people who were caught up with the self-syndrome? It's all about you, your time, and your plans. Yet there is a generation that is falling apart from the inside out. Who will reach out to Peter?

> *And they said to me, "the survivors who left from the*
> *captivity in the province are there in great distress*
> *and reproach. The wall of Jerusalem is also broken*
> *down, and its gates are burned with fire." So it was,*
> *when I heard these words, that I sat down and wept,*
> *and mourned for many days, I was fasting and pray-*
> *ing before the God of heaven*
> *(Nehemiah 1:3-4.)*

After hearing that the wall of Jerusalem was in shambles,

Nehemiah didn't sit and criticize the pastor or youth pastor. He didn't say,"See, no one ever gets things done around here." Many times as young people, it is a lot easier to sit back and criticize why something is not getting done, rather than stepping out and doing it yourself.

There is a story of a soda can that was in the church parking lot for several days. As church members drove up to the church, they looked at the can and complained, "The committee hasn't delegated anyone to pick up trash in the parking lot yet?" Soon the talk about the soda can spread throughout the congregation. Finally, one Sunday after Sunday School, a little girl saw the can, picked it up and threw it in the garbage. This story sounds silly, but some of us do the same thing. We wait for others to start a ministry or tend to the needs of the church while we don't do anything but criticize.

Don't wait for anyone to start an evangelism team. If you feel led and the pastor gives his permission, then go for it. Nehemiah felt a burden, and with that burden came tears and consecration. Peter's generation will not affect you unless you go to group homes; read the obituary section of a young person putting an end to their life; or hear the news of a young child killing his or her parents. See if that will not break your heart. Vision is birthed into reality through tears and compassion. You need to feel for the lost. You have to go to sleep praying for them and waking up thinking how you can make a difference.

Nehemiah asked King Artaxerxes if he could go to his hometown and rebuild the walls. Nehemiah left a good, secure job of being a cupbearer, to go do manual labor. A vision and passion will take you places you would have never attempted to go. Visionaries are those who will put others before themselves. For Nehemiah, it wasn't about his 401k package or the means to buy the latest gadgets. It was about the security of his people, it was all about Peter.

Today what consumes you? Are you like the girl whose life revolves around a man? Or are material things in life your priority? What about finding your place in society? While Peter is crying for help, we have lost the most important key for vision and that is to reach out to the lost. When was the last time you cried for a soul? When was the last time you envisioned hell? When was the last time you got so disgusted with sin? Peter's generation is crying out to us, do you hear their voices? Can you feel their damp pillows filled with tears? God wants to give us a vision to reach out to Peter's generation.

While you're depressed because your girlfriend broke up with you, the other girl bought the same outfit as you, you can't afford the latest gadget, or your parents gave you a curfew, Peter's generation is lost. What about those kids who won't see their mother or father again? What about the children who are sleeping in a car tonight with their family? What about the young boy who is seeing his father beat his mother? While we're caught up with the self-syndrome, we are losing Peter's generation. God is looking for visionaries that can reach Peter's generation before it is too late.

HOW CAN WE REACH THEM?

If my people, which are called by my name, shall humble themselves, and pray, and seek my face, and turn from the wicked ways; then I will hear from heaven, and will forgive their sin, and will heal their land.
—*2 Chronicles 7:14*

When was the last time you went to a homeless shelter, city park, or a local low-income apartment complex and felt such a burden for the people deceived by the enemy's lies? When was the last time you cried for Peter's generation? Not just a tear, but like Nehemiah, fell on your face moaning and groaning, interceding for the lost. God is calling us once again, to leave our comfort zone. Just like Nehemiah left the king's palace to go and rebuild the walls that had been destroyed, will you leave your comfort zone and go to that girl that was molested at a young age? Will you go to that boy who gets beat by his drug-addicted mother? Will you go for Peter?

To reach out to Peter is the purpose for your existence. Maybe you have been through hard times in your life. Maybe you feel like you're an accident and useless, but God thinks differently. You are special and useful for His kingdom and today God wants to use everything that you have been through to reach out to Peter's generation.

We need to humble ourselves, fall on our faces and cry out for this generation. We need to rid ourselves from temporal pleasures (like the sand in the container) and do something that will benefit God's kingdom.

THINGS YOU CAN DO:

- Go to a local homeless shelter.
- Visit a runaway home for teenagers.
- Tell someone about Christ no matter how they look and where they come from.
- Start a mentorship program at your local church in which you can reach out to the kids in your community through sports, skits, and free food.
- Instead of going to eat at an expensive restaurant, invite someone at your church who is less fortunate and take them out to eat.

Chapter 9

NORM DOESN'T LIVE HERE

Justin was once passionate about his relationship with God. In church his hands would be lifted high, focusing on the greatness of God. He didn't seem to mind the other dead folks around him. One day after school, while doing his homework, he heard a knock at the door, so he ran downstairs. An unfamiliar voice said, "Hi, my name is Norm. Can I come in?"

Justin did wrong by allowing Norm into his house that day. Soon Justin and Norm became good friends and were inseparable. Even though Norm had moved in, Justin's parents never met him. Soon Justin was skipping youth service and mid-week prayer, and was caught up with video games and trying to fit in with the crowd he always seemed to ignore at school. During Sunday service, Justin began assimilating with the dead crowd, frequently conversing with Norm, "Well if they're not going to praise God, why should I?" Soon Norm dictated everything Justin could or could not do. Justin now fit in with the status quo of doing nothing for God. He did not have an identity anymore since he was whatever Norm said he was. Could Justin escape Norm? Being that Norm wasn't human, it wasn't going to be an easy task. Norm was a spirit of being normal, ordinary – the norm.

The spirit that Justin let into his life that day, when he opened the door of his heart, was what killed the drive and the desire he had to serve God.

Norm influences people to fall into the same routine on a daily basis. He makes people comfortable. He makes people average. With Norm in control, everything is mechanical. Wake up, eat, go to work, come home, and go to sleep. Understand that I am not saying that having a schedule is wrong because I too have to be on a schedule. However, you cannot allow programs, schedules, or society to dictate every moment of your day. If so, you will become a clone of what your parents want you to be and what society says you should become.

Society says if you don't make a certain amount of money, you're useless. The media says that if you don't look a certain way, then you're ugly. Some parents pressure their children into doing something they may not necessarily want to do, so the children unhappily try to live up to their parents' expectations. If we allow people to dictate our decision making, we will live a life of frustration.

Out of the billions of people here on earth, God made you different. No one on the face of this earth has the same fingerprint. God designed you to be special from everyone else. He never wanted two people to be alike. The only thing people have in common is when they come to the knowledge of Jesus Christ and are changed through the power of the blood that was shed on Calvary.

Someone once said, "the enemy of best is good." It is being comfortable in the place we are at right now, that keeps us from moving forward. Perhaps it is reflecting over our past accomplishments that keep us content and stagnant. We feel like graduating from high school, having received Christ in our life, or receiving a job promotion is good enough. The question we should ask ourselves is, "What have I done since?" Often we are easily satisfied with our achievements, and instead of reaching for a higher goal, we end up settling for Norm. However, the apostle Paul says we should move *"from glory to glory."* God does not want us to repeat each day like yesterday. In order for us to grow in God, we need to make spiritual advancements. Visionaries aren't comfortable with what they've done but search for new mountains to climb and more victories to experience.

Visionaries are those who refuse to live only by yesterday's accomplishments- they anticipate today's victories.

At times Norm will come in and tell you you're fine the way you are. He will tell you to stop praying and reading the Word of God because he knows it will weaken your spirit, making you an easy target for the enemy. That is why you need to watch out for Norm because he will destroy you. If you are reading this book and have had your share of disappointments with family, friends, and society, it is important that you don't listen to Norm. He will tell you that you will be just like your negative mom or drunken dad, and if you believe him, you will become like your parents. Don't let your situations dictate your future. Instead, follow the vision and plan that God has for your life.

Let me introduce you to someone who didn't follow Norm no matter what her situation looked like. Harriet Tubman, an African American of the South, was born during the 1800's when it was the norm for African Americans to be slaves. Growing up she had no control over her situation and had to fulfill tasks that were usually assigned to adults. If she fell short of accomplishing a task, she was gruesomely beaten. One of her main responsibilities, for example, was to care for her masters' infant son. She had to stay awake every night to assure that the baby wouldn't cry and wake his mother. If she fell asleep, Harriet would get brutally whipped as a punishment. Even though society marked her a slave, Harriet knew in her heart that she should be a free woman. Therefore, she went beyond the norm, beyond her conditions of living. Knowing the consequences of getting caught was death, Tubman was determined to achieve her freedom. Putting all fear aside, she went in search of the Underground Railroad and ultimately escaped the norm. Harriet Tubman didn't stop there. She returned to the South countless times, in an effort to lead hundreds more to freedom.

In her heart there was a dream. A dream of running down a green pasture; free. A dream of raising children; free. A dream of living; free. Because of her determination and refusal to settle with the norm of society, she was able to realize her dream of freedom.

Today God is looking for visionaries who refuse to be part of the status quo. They know in their hearts that God has something powerful and great in store for their life. Visionaries refuse to accept the current circumstances as they are. Instead, they have hope for tomorrow. They refuse to allow society to dictate who they are and what they will become.

One afternoon when I finished preaching, a lady came up to me and thanked me for the message. She began to tell me that her father was a child molester and instead of helping, her mother would constantly lash out and accuse her of being just like her dad. After years of this mental abuse, she believed her mother and felt worthless. During the preaching, though, she received a word from God telling her she was not like her physical father but like her Spiritual Father. From that moment on, her wounds began to heal and her mind was transformed. I believe the next time she sees her mother she will tell her, "I'm not going to listen to you anymore. I've listened to you all my life and let you dictate what I would be. But not anymore! I am not who you said I was. I am special in the eyes of God, even though you didn't think so."

There is a story about a young man whose father died when he was a little boy. In Brooklyn, NY, where he was raised, the majority of men in his neighborhood either died young or went to prison. With all the odds stacked against him, he chose to rise above the norm. He was determined that he was not going to be another statistic. While his environment was infested with gangs, women, and drugs, he knew that he was a psalmist, and he loved God with all of his heart. Because he was steadfast in his belief and refused to be a clone of society, years later he became the founder of the Love Fellowship Crusade Choir. This man has taken gospel music to another level. His name is Hezekiah Walker.

History is made up of individuals who dared to challenge and exceed the norm.

- Neither the water nor the frightened disciples hindered Peter from stepping out of the boat and onto the sea. While it was against the laws of nature for a man to walk on water, Peter refused to let this opportunity go by and boldly asked Jesus if he could walk out toward Him.

- While the land of promise seemed impossible to conquer in the eyes of most men, Joshua and Caleb rose above the intimidating words of the spies and the complaints of the congregation. With unwavering faith he told Moses, "We can do it. Let us go and possess the land of promise."
- Nehemiah refused to see the destruction of his people and city, so he rose up and gathered some of them to help rebuild the walls of Jerusalem despite being ridiculed and intimidated by the enemy. Visionaries rise above the norm by stepping out in faith and taking risks, as these men have shown. They were willing to walk on water even though it was against the laws of nature, seize the land in spite of opposition, and leave a secure job to do what no one else wanted to do. Visionaries know that something great resides in them, and they don't allow Norm in their hearts. If you want to be a visionary, you've got to refuse to live in mediocrity. You must be willing to take a risk.

YOU MUST BE WILLING TO:

- Praise God even if no one else wants to.
- Evangelize even if others don't want to.
- Refuse to settle with the status quo.
- Dream.

You need to tell Norm to get out of your life and begin living at the level God called you to. David continually rose above the norm throughout his life. One day, while bringing his brothers a sack lunch, he found that a Philistine was threatening the armies of Israel. As David looked around, he saw a band of fearful men. Norm had set in. No one wanted to confront this giant warrior by the name of Goliath because they were afraid to take a risk. But something always happens when a visionary comes into a setting where Norm resides. A visionary who has a relationship with God, knows that not even a giant can stop him. David was this type of young man. When he arrived at the scene, he bravely said, "Let me fight this giant."

There are giants that will try to intimidate your youth group by making you believe that you can't grow numerically or that there will never be revival. There are some carnal giants in your youth group that like to gossip and bicker. Because no one is willing to risk taking a stand, the baptistery is dry, the worship is drier, and the people of God are just dead. But when a visionary steps in, they look at the giant and say, "It's time for you to go!" They look around and they have their own praise party. You know why? They refuse to let Norm dictate their actions. They understand that *"When the enemy comes in like a flood the Lord shall lift up a standard against him."*

There is a story about a missionary's wife who saved $50 for Christmas presents for her children. While she was at the store, a thief came running by and stole her purse. This timid lady, who never spoke unless she had to, saw this man run off with her purse. She became infuriated because she had saved every spare penny throughout the year to buy presents for Christmas. She took off her shoes in the store and ran after the thief. Soon the thief heard someone screaming loudly and as he turned around, he discovered it was the missionary lady running behind him at full speed. As he was about to exit the store, two well-fed ladies were blocking the door, enabling the missionary's wife to catch up to him. She quickly grabbed her purse and screamed, "IT'S MINE!"

That is what some of you need to do today. You need to tell Norm to get his ugly hands off of your life. Tell him you will not listen to his lies anymore. You are beautiful, not ugly. You are smart, not dumb. You have a future, you're anointed, you are the elect of God and you're victorious. You need to say, "You can't dictate my life anymore, Norm. I'll praise God at all times. I will tell someone about God wherever I go. I am not your slave, but I am free."

Who the son is set free is free indeed (John 8:36).

THIS WEEK DO SOMETHING YOU NORMALLY DO NOT DO:

- Tell someone that Jesus loves him or her regardless of where you are (McDonald's, Wal-Mart, or school).
- Give someone money, a card, or something else that costs you.
- Praise God with your hands, voice and feet.
- Volunteer at a homeless shelter or food bank.

Chapter 10

MOVERS AND PUSHERS

*And Joshua said unto the Children of Israel, come hither, and hear
the words of the Lord your God. And Joshua said, hereby ye shall
know that the living God is among you, and that he will without
fail drive out from before you the Canaanites,
and the Hittites, and the Hivites, and the Perizzites,
and the Girgashites, and the Amorites,
and the Jebusites.*
Joshua 3:9-10

When you attend a football game, the momentum of the crowd
is so thick you can cut it with a knife. The cheerleaders are
cheering, the music is playing and the mascot is doing cartwheels.
All of this is geared toward getting the fans hyped up for the game.

Momentum is the power to create movement.[8]

The result of momentum is great expectation, joy, and team-
work. When a team has momentum to win the game, they will automatically work together and have lots of fun playing.

Vision gives us spiritual momentum, which results in spiritual
advancement. A football team's goal, or vision, is to win, and
momentum provides the rush for them to achieve that goal. The

same is true with God's purpose for your life. When you receive a vision for what you are supposed to do, it will produce momentum for you to get there. Our ultimate hope, as children of God, is to one day see Him face to face and live with Him throughout eternity. This vision is what triggers a momentum within us to live a godly life and work for the Lord.

Momentum is what fuels vision to get to your destiny.

"Heaven is miles before me. How am I going to get there?" you ask. This is where vision comes in. It produces the momentum you need to see your vision become a reality. Momentum also gives you the energy and strength to endure the setbacks that you may face. Today I ask you, "Do you have enough momentum to keep you running toward the prize?" If you don't, you may burn out which will prohibit you from advancing spiritually. Being tired and weak can bring negative consequences that may be the cause of a great defeat. What would happen if a football team got tired and had no strength left to draw from before the game was over? Could they still win the game? Probably not. Yet today, there are many young people who have run out of momentum and have become weary and discouraged. When their priorities are out of order, they leave no room for God or their spiritual advancement. In order to reach our vision, we must progress not regress.

When someone replaces spiritual momentum for their own energy, eventually they will get fatigued and die out. As a result, they lose their joy, and it then becomes easy for them to stop running this Christian race. I hope that there is a youth pastor, a youth leader, or a young person who refuses to give up the vision, someone willing to encourage young people not to stop dreaming. I pray that there are movers and pushers who will motivate others to keep serving God.

Do you ever find yourself at the beginning of the year or after a youth camp having the energy and desire to soul win and be a better Christian, but as the year progresses you aren't as motivated? Does your youth group go through spurts of revival and dedication then fall back to their complacent lifestyle? King David experienced something similar to this in 1 Samuel chapter thirty when the Amalekites came into Ziklag and took all of his soldiers' families, including his. Once the men heard that the Lord wanted them to pursue the enemy, a great momentum arose among them to subdue the enemy. Immediately, six hundred men bravely marched toward the enemy's camp. However, in verses nine and ten, we find that two hundred men stayed behind because they were faint. I am sure that all of the other soldiers, including David, were tired and faint, but what made the difference was they had their eyes on the goal. This is what motivated them to continue marching. David could have given up at this point and said, "Two hundred men can't march, so we can't do this." However, the Bible says in verse ten that David pursued.

Regardless of what goes on in your youth group, you need to keep marching toward your goal. Inspite of the obstacles that may come against your youth group, you need to pursue after what God has shown you. Because David was a mover and pusher who encouraged the remaining men, they pursued and recovered everything that the enemy had stolen.

In this hour, God is looking for movers and pushers that can stand and lead this generation to the place where God wants them. You must make up your mind to be a visionary, who will stand up, motivate and inspire other young people to finish the task that God has called them to do. Be a mover and pusher. I guarantee that you will be faced with questions, insecurities and obstacles, but I also guarantee that when you step out, God will also step out because *"He is able to do exceeding, abundantly above all that we could ask or think according to the power that worketh in us" (Ephesians 3:20).*

A mover and pusher is one who encourages. He or she understands that encouragement is not only effective, but needed because many young people lack self-esteem. Others are looking for someone to encourage them and let them know they are not alone if they stand up for the gospel. A kind word or a card can uplift someone who is trying to make a difference in the kingdom of God. Sending a card or calling someone who has missed church for example, can be an effective encouragement tool.

Right now as you read this chapter, someone is cheering you on.

King David is telling you that your financial status is of no concern to God. His eyes are fixed solely on your heart. King David is telling you that it matters not what position your parents may or may not have in the church. God called a young shepherd boy one day and anointed him king of Israel.

I hear Rahab telling someone that even though your parents aren't living God, you must continue to faithfully serve Him despite your situation. Rahab says, "You see, I wasn't raised in church. I didn't even know the God you serve, but when I first heard about His power, I believed in Him and He saved my family and I. Generations later, Jesus came to Earth through my lineage."

I hear Paul telling you that no matter how bad you have failed God, He is longing to change you if you respond to Him. He desires to use you in areas you cannot even imagine.

Youth leader, can you hear the sound of the thunderous applause of saints cheering you on? Can you hear the loving voice of the God of heaven and earth saying, "I believe in you, and have entrusted you to carry out My work?" Now you must do the same for someone who is insecure and needs a push to do what God has called them to do. Go ahead. Be a mover and pusher. Cheer someone on because all heaven is cheering you on.

> *Wherefore seeing we also are compassed about with so great a cloud of witnesses, let us lay aside every weight, and the sin which doth easily beset us, and let us run with patience the race that is set before us. Looking unto Jesus the author and finisher of our faith...*
>
> *Hebrews 12:1*

I wrote this book to remind you that God is not done with you. He just began working in you. There is a great work that God has assigned you to accomplish, and I'm here to push you into a new realm of the spirit, which you have not seen.

> *Remember the word which Moses the servant of the Lord commanded you, saying, the Lord your God*

hath given you rest, and hath given you this land
Joshua 1:13

Joshua called a general meeting to remind the people of Israel about their promise, a land flowing with milk and honey. He was convinced that God was going to do something miraculous. Joshua remembered when Moses was leading the people toward the promise land and how they wandered in the wilderness for forty years because of their grasshopper mentality. He remembered the visionless people that hindered God's plan. Convinced that this was not going to happen again, Joshua's vision produced momentum within the congregation to conquer the promise land. Joshua was a mover and pusher.

God is looking for movers and pushers that can push young people to do something great for Him. Can it be done? Yes it can. All God needs is one young person to influence and lead others to a place of greatness in God - a young person who will remind and encourage others to believe God's promises for their life.

HOW CAN I BE A MOVER AND PUSHER?

Let no man despise thy youth; but be thou an exam-
ple of the believers, in word, in conversation, in
charity, in spirit, in faith, in purity. Till I come give
attendance to reading, to exhortation, to doctrine.
Neglect not the gift that is in thee...
1 Timothy 4:12-14

This generation needs "now" young people that will fight for their God given vision and anointing. It needs young people who will not let grasshoppers devour their joy and harvest. God is looking for "now" young people who will encourage others to start living out their life the way He has intended.

You have what this generation is looking for. People are tired of others letting them down. They want someone to look up to and receive direction from. This is where you must step in. Your conduct and testimony are vital because people are looking to follow someone who is real. They want to follow someone who is a true motivator - a true mover and pusher.

Joshua had established himself well. He was dedicated and faithful to Moses. He was one who came back with a good report. His experience and testimony impacted others to follow him. Before we can push young people into ministry, we need to be involved in ministry. If we want young people to pray and read the Word of God, we must pray and read the Word of God. Before we can push others into doing something, we must first set the example. This is a requirement for being a visionary

As a youth pastor, I strongly believe 1 Timothy 4:12-14 is essential in order to be an effective mover and pusher. Daily, I encourage young people to develop a personal relationship with God that is necessary in order to stir up the gift that is within them. I too get tired at times with having to follow a busy schedule and with quenching the fiery arrows of Satan. However, I draw my strength from the Lord, first of all, and from all of the young people that come to our mid-week life lessons. When I see faithful young people who serve God without the support of a family, it motivates me to praise God all the more. You don't know how many people you encourage by being yourself. It may be your faithfulness or conduct that encourages others. Whatever it is, someone is looking up to you and is being ministered to by you.

Reach out to someone in your youth group today and tell them to continue pressing on. Tell them that they will make it, and God's plan will make them laugh when it is all said and done. We need young people to encourage others to continue serving God. One of the compliments I get from young people I oversee at Jubilee Center is that even when they didn't want to serve God, I was always there to encourage them to come to church and dedicate their lives to God. Each of us needs someone to remind us to stir up the gift that is within us because sometimes we can get so caught up with life that we need to be reminded where we are going. Are you that one that can move and push people out of their comfort zone and into their destiny? Give it a try. Remember that someone is cheering you on.

Chapter 11

YOUR STORY IS JUST BEGINNING

*Write the vision, and make it plain upon tables, that
he may run that readeth it. For the vision is yet for
an appointed time, but at the end it shall speak, and
not lie: though it tarry, wait for it; because it will
surely come, it will not tarry.*
Habakkuk 2:2-3

As I look over the last ten years I've been involved in youth
ministry, I am amazed by how much I've matured in God, yet
I realized I still have room for growth. I a I have progressed in my
Christian walk ever since the call of God in my room. I don't know
where I would be today had I not heeded the call, but by the grace
of God I have come thus far.

"Have there been failures, Ben?" you ask. Yes, and there have
also been great victories. If it wasn't for the encounter I had with
God that day, I don't know if I would be as focused on the vision as
I am today. What I saw in that vision finally came to pass two years
after I appointed a highly qualified choir director. I believe when I
transferred the directing of the youth choir, God launched me into
another phase of ministry. Even though I never saw the entire
fulfillment of the vision while directing the youth choir, I believe I

was a tool whom God used to pave the way.

Although Moses never entered into the promise land, he is an example of on who paved the way for the children of Israel. As a result, they experienced freedom and had a land they could call their own. In like manner, God uses different people to start up something for his Glory. Will you make yourself available?

Though I am no longer serving in the capacity as youth choir director, God has allowed me to step into a higher level of ministry. Currently I am the youth pastor at Jubilee Center in Modesto, California. The Lord has blessed me with a beautiful wife and two handsome sons. In addition, He has given me the awesome opportunity to lead wonderful young people closer to God. What can I say about the AJC Krew? They are the best youth group a church could ever have. Ten ministries have developed from this youth group. Why? Because they understand that the purpose for their existence is to reach "Peter's generation." I hope as you conclude this final chapter, excuses don't hinder you from living out your God-given purpose. Remember it only takes one. One that is tired of living a life with "Norm." One who can cause a flame of passion to ignite an entire youth group. It takes only one visionary to turn things around. Will you be that visionary? If so, I want to leave you with six important steps that guide you in becoming a visionary.

1. Pray

Some of you will probably ask, "Why doesn't God show me anything for my life?" The answer is probably because you are not taking time out of your busy schedule for God to show you what He has in store for you. This is why you need to develop a daily prayer time with God. You need to ask Him to reveal His will for your life. When we pray, we become more sensitive spiritually, which allows us to see things in the spiritual realm that we wouldn't see otherwise. In your prayer time, ask God to reveal your purpose here on earth as clear as possible.

There are three steps that can help make your prayer time successful. The first is: **find time to be alone with God**. I prefer the morning time because it is the quietest time in my day. Jesus also preferred the morning:

Now in the morning, having risen a long while
before daylight, He went out and departed to a soli-
tary place; and there He prayed.

Mark 1:35

King David also preferred morning devotion:

In the morning, O LORD , you hear my voice; in the
morning I lay my requests before you and wait in
expectation.

Psalms 5:3

The second step to help make your prayer time successful is:
find a place to meet with God.

Jesus went out as usual to the Mount of Olives, and
his disciples followed him.

Luke 22: 39

Find a place where you know you can focus on God and where
He can speak to you. It can be in your room, in your backyard, or
anywhere you may choose. The place that you select will be your
meeting place with Him. Regardless of the time you choose, He is
sure to meet you there daily. In times of dire need, you will find
yourself running to this secret place to pray.

Last, during your prayer time, I encourage you to **play soft**
prayer music to prepare your heart and spirit.

Open my eyes, that I may see your wondrous things
from your law.

Psalms 119:18

You need to make sure the music is not blaring in your ears,
distracting you from focusing on God. Prayer music can usher one's
spirit into the presence of God.

2. Write

When God shows you something in the spirit, you must immediately write it down, otherwise you will forget it. The Bible says, *"Write the vision, and make it plain..." (Habakkuk 2:2).*

Therefore, you need to write it out so you may understand what God is saying to you. If God is calling you to start a coat ministry, write it down and start seeing the vision as you put it on paper. Remember, God will give you the strength and resources to carry out your purpose.

3. Tell your pastor

It is really important to share what God has spoken to you about with your pastor. God has placed a pastor to guide and feed His sheep. Your pastor must be informed because God is a God of order and if your desire is contrary to the pastor's, then you need to submit yourself with the vision God has given the man of God. Ask him if this is something he could see you doing. Seek his advice, and also ask him to pray with you.

David had been anointed by the Prophet Samuel to be king of Israel, only there was a problem. There was already a king. David had many opportunities to kill Saul but refused to touch the anointed of God. Your Pastor may not be the most innovative person and you probably have greater ideas for the church, but remember God has placed him as pastor and he knows what's best for the church. God is looking at our obedience above anything else. His Word says, "Obedience is greater than sacrifice" (1 Samuel 15:22). God demands our obedience before any sacrifice we may offer Him because He is a God of order. Always remember that as long as we obey His Word above all other desires, His blessing will be upon us. In due season, He will elevate us to the place we ought to be.

One of the problems today is that there are some young men that are wet behind the ears, per se, who want to run 500 miles with an idea without consulting their pastor. They need to remember that although they are young and energetic, they do not have the experience their pastor has, nor do they have the insights that the pastor's experience has to offer. We must all learn to submit to our pastor's vision in order to be blessed by God.

4. Be mentored

You need to find a mover and pusher that will help you fulfill the call. A mentor is needed because you will learn much from their experience in serving God. They should keep you accountable to your gift and calling. A mentor can be your pastor, a youth pastor, or another spiritually grounded person. Joshua, for example, was mentored by Moses. Joshua looked up to and followed Moses everywhere he went. He was there when Moses would pray (Exodus 33:11) He was at battle when his mentor was at battle (Exodus 17). Joshua gained experience, growth, and wisdom by following Moses. Elisha walked and served Elijah everywhere he went. As a result, Elisha received a double portion of his mentor's spirit. We must find a mentor that will help us and inspire us to live out our call.

5. Make sure it compliments you

When God called Moses to lead His people, He didn't tell Him to go to a Bible College and major in Public Speaking because of his speaking limitations. God did, however, require him to be himself. God promised to raise men around him to do what he couldn't do. God is not going to call you to do something that you don't have the ability to do. He will only draw from the strengths and talents that He has given you. Remember, if you haven't received compliments you on your singing, then you should think twice about choosing singing as your ministry. God will never demand more from you. He is willing and waiting to use what you have right now.

6. Run with it, destiny awaits

Once you've prayed about what God has shown you and your pastor gives you his support, you need to run with the vision. You can't procrastinate until tomorrow. You've read in this book that there are no excuses good enough to keep you from doing what God has called you to do. You can't be like Leo and take the precious gifts God has given you for granted. The fact that you woke up this morning is proof that God has entrusted you to carry out a mission. What an awesome privilege! Go ahead, Peter is waiting for you. When it is all said and done, God's purpose for your life will make you laugh.

Chapter 12

WHAT'S YOUR STORY

Everyone has a story. While some chapters may contain joyous occasions filled with laughter and success, others may be filled with pain and setbacks. Whether positive or negative, every experience in life has a valuable lesson. Through some experiences our faith and trust in God have increased. Other experiences serve as testimonies of the power and wisdom of God. These can be effective not only for personal edification, but also for the edification of others who may be going through a similar situation. Here are some of these stories...

KIMBERLI

A few years ago, Donnie McClurkin sang a song entitled *I'll Trust you, Lord!* The words of the song have forever been engraved in my mind:

> ...What if it hurts? I'll trust you Lord. What if you cry? I'll trust you Lord. What if it doesn't work the first time that you try? I'll trust you Lord. What if you call my name...I'll trust you Lord. And don't feel me near? I'll trust you Lord...

The words have spoken true in my life and all I have been

through. If you were to look at me during a church service, you might assume that I have a perfect life. I sit in the front, I lift my hands freely in worship, I pay close attention to the preaching, I pray with the young girls at the altar, I smile and converse after the service is over. My life from the outside seems perfect. Once you move past the outward appearance though, and look inside of me, you will see all that I have gone through in the past seven years. You will see that I have not had a perfect life. I don't lead a life that is always full of roses. In fact, there have been times when my life was very difficult.

I grew up in a Christian home. Every Sunday, I can recall getting ready in the morning and then piling up in our car and making the trip to church. Every night before dinner and before bed, my father would gather the family together and we would say our prayers. I grew up learning about God, and hearing the familiar Bible stories one is told in Sunday school. Despite all of this though, I did not know God. It was all a routine to me: go to church every Wednesday and Sunday, pray before you eat, pray before you go to sleep, and try to read the Bible occasionally. Although I knew all of that, I didn't make it a lifestyle like I should have.

When I went to high school and got older, I wasn't forced to go to church anymore. Our family no longer ate together, and the routine of family bedtime prayer had stopped as well. I wouldn't say I drifted away from God because I never really had an active relationship with Him. During my junior year of high school, I really began evaluating my life and checking my priorities. One thing that I believed needed change was my relationship with God. I knew that while I claimed to be a Christian, my walk with God was non-existent. It was at this time that a friend from work invited me to church with him. Eventually in the course of a year, I made that commitment to actually serve God and live for Him.

This decision though, would cost me a lot in the years to come. My father, who is such an awesome man, raised me a certain way, believing certain things, and the fact that I was going to a church that had different views on certain issues did not make him happy. I could see how much my choice disappointed him. It hurt to see how he believed that somehow along the way he had failed in raising me.

In my senior year of high school and three months after I was baptized my parents decided that our family was going to move. So here I was: an extremely shy person, a disappointment to my father, and a baby in the Lord moving to an area where I knew no one. It was extremely hard. I was all alone. While in my hometown I had friends who were my support system when I was going through things with my family, it was just me in this new city.

I can vividly remember and am still emotional when I think about all I went through with my family. It was so hard and I felt like God deserted me at times. I can recall crying myself to sleep at night so many times, and crying out to God to give me strength. I remember telling Him I couldn't make it another day unless I knew He was right beside me. You see, I was a daddy's girl. I was the child that always got good grades, I was the one who stayed out of trouble, I was the responsible one. While my sister got pregnant right out of high school and my brother was always in trouble at school, I was the good one. But all that changed with my decision to serve God. I now became the disappointment, the failure, the outsider, and it was so hard.

For years I hated to be in the same room as my father because I did not know what comment he would make about my church. I would come home after an awesome service and have to run straight to my room so no one could see my red eyes from crying. I would leave church at night so distraught because I wanted a family where I could go and talk about what was preached that night, but I knew that family did not exist for me because my father just did not agree. I remember him telling me how he did not want me to go to my church and how everything I believed was wrong. It hurt so much. I could see in his eyes how much it hurt him that I believed what I did, and I was devastated. Our relationship was ruined for a few years because I avoided him, and I knew he did not agree with the choices I was making. So many times I would want to just cry out to God in my room and speak in tongues but I couldn't. I would have to turn my music on and bury myself in my pillow and cry. If it wasn't bad enough that my dad did not like my lifestyle, my brother and sister constantly made fun of me. Not only that, but at every family gathering, I was the outsider. The one who didn't drink, the one who didn't party, the one who didn't wear makeup…the list goes on. Here I was seventeen, eighteen, nineteen, twenty years old, and my life was so full of pain.

It would have been so easy for me to give up. I know it would have made my parents happy, and it would have saved me ridicule. The only thing that kept me going was God. He was by my side every step of the way. Those nights where I would lay in my bed for hours crying and calling out to Him wondering when all the pain would go away; He was there. The days where I would lay all my burdens at the altar telling Him I didn't know how I would make it; He was there. When my family was making fun of me; He was there. When my dad was telling me how wrong I was; He was there. He was there for me when no one else was. He knew the pain I was experiencing when every one else thought I was happy. He never left me, and I was determined never to leave Him.

People may look at me now and say, "Kimberli, you praise God to much." "Kimberli, you pray too much." "Kimberli, you are at church too much." If they only partially understood all I had to go through to get where I am right now, then they would understand. So many times I see people who have been raised in church act like it is no big deal not to serve God with all their heart. I see them come to church when they want, lift their hands when they want, and it frustrates me because it is a struggle for me to come to church. Not a spiritual struggle, but an actual struggle. Although my relationship with my family is a lot better now that I am older, I dread the day my dad is going to say something negative to me, or let me know how he really does not want me to go to my church anymore. Because of this, it is not easy for me to come to church. When I said that I would serve God until the day I died, I meant it. I will continue praising God with all I have because I know what it is like to live in a home where your siblings make fun of your Christian music. I will continue to pray as much as I possibly can at church because I know what it is like to not be able to speak in tongues in my own home. I will continue to go to church whenever there is a service because there will probably be a day when my father will tell me he doesn't want me to go anymore, and I will have to make that decision to keep going anyway.

I look at my life now and all that I have been able to do, and I am amazed. Every day in prayer, I think of where God has brought me, and tears flow freely from my face. I think of the conferences I have given, the Bible studies I have led, the words of encouragement I have been able to tell another young person, and the prayer ministry that I am in charge of. It leaves me speechless. I am not in any way listing my accomplishments to boast, I am saying them because I see God's hand upon me with every step I have taken. I never let my circumstances stand in the way of praising God. I never use the fact that I come to church by myself as an excuse not to be active.

I can honestly say I am thankful for all the pain I went through, all the tears that I have shed, all the heartache I was dealt. I see the relationship I have with God and I know it was cultivated because of those experiences. I wasn't able to depend on anyone else, so I was forced to depend solely on God. I did not have a dad I could ask a Biblical question to. I did not have a mom I could go to for advice. I did not have a sister I could pray with. I had only God to turn to. Seven years after I decided to make serving God my lifestyle, I am thankful to Him for everything.

I know I am no one special, but I realize you don't have to be the pastor's daughter to be used by God. You don't have to be the choir director's son for God to do something in your life. In fact, if you look at many people in the Bible, they do not come from the best family backgrounds. The Bible says that Josiah's father, Amon, and his grandfather, Manasseh, both did evil in the sight of the Lord, but Josiah determined in his mind that he was going to live for God anyway. David was just a shepherd boy, but God raised him to be king. Ruth's parents were Moabites, yet it was through her lineage that Jesus would be born. Esther was an orphan, yet God used her to save her people. These were all people who did not let their circumstances, or their family history dictate their future. The same can be said for everyone else. In I Samuel 16:7, God tells Samuel that He does not look at the outward appearance as man does, rather he looks at the heart of the person. I live off this scripture. While people may say, "Why is Kim giving conferences, her parents don't even come to church?" Or, "Why is Kim leading Partners in Prayer, she can't even speak in tongues in her own home?" Or "Why does Kim have a scholarship to college, her parents didn't even go to college?" Or "Why is Kim going to go to the mission field, her dad is not a pastor?" God is saying, "While you look at the outward appearance, I am looking at a heart that desires to be in my presence more than anything. I am looking at a girl who would give up her education in a second, if it meant doing my will. I am looking at a girl who despite getting ridiculed by her family continued serving me. I am looking at a girl..."

I did not say all that to make myself look good, but I am saying that I had to make so many sacrifices when it came to serving God. I could have chosen the easy route. I could have given up and people might have understood, but I chose to place God first in my life. I chose to live for him no matter the consequences. I chose to give my all to Him, not looking for reward, not looking for recognition, not looking for acclaim. I just wanted to serve Him. In life we have to make choices. There will come a time when you have to decide how you are going to live for God. Are you going to let whatever circumstances you had to endure keep you from giving God your all, or are you going to serve God with all your heart, mind and soul? I chose to serve Him with everything.

- Kim, is a dynamic young lady who leads Partner in Prayer, a morning prayer held at Jubilee Center. Kim is a speaker who ministers powerfully to young ladies about prayer, a passion for God, and godly living. She is highly respected among the youth group and is a great inspiration.

MATTHEW

"Cancer, how could this be?" I asked myself. My father, friend and mentor had been diagnosed with Hodgkins lymphoma. I was mentally numb. Being a youth leader at my local church I always encouraged young people to love God and remain faithful to his promises. But now I found myself at a crossroad of my faith. I found myself like a boxer who was down for the count, my opponent had knocked all the breath out of me.

While my face was on the floor for the count, the enemy was whispering in my ear "Your dad is going to die", "Just give up your faith in God", and "How can you praise God when your dad has cancer?" As I was on the floor refusing to get up and confront this trial, I all of a sudden experienced God's hand reach out to me and say, "Get up, this battle is not yours it's mine." With all the strength I had I immediately arose and continued to battle this enemy of cancer.

I want to encourage a young person who is reading this book and is using a traumatic situation like mine as an excuse why God can't use them. As for myself I continued to stay in the ring and fight with my father this enemy called cancer. And I remained faithful in my youth leader responsibilities and leading worship on Sundays. Yes, my father's ordeal was hard and full of pain but the calling God had placed on my life was greater for me to fulfill. As I continued to be faithful to God, he was faithful to me. God has extended my fathers life and granted us time together once again. My father and mother celebrated twenty-seven years of marriage and his fiftieth birthday. As of today, my father is alive and is still ministering in song.

We are survivors. We have survived three battles with cancer and many oppositions. God has been faithful to us and I know God can be faithful to you and your situation. No matter what you go through do not wait for your circumstance to change but step out and be used of God and know that "No weapon that is formed against thee shall prosper..." Isaiah 54:17

- Matt is the minister of music at Jubilee Center, he is a dynamic worship leader and song writer. He is also a youth leader and choir director of the AJC youth choir who has traveled to various places ministering to young people.

CECIL

Growing up in South Side Modesto a lot of things can happen to a teenager who is searching for fulfillment for his/her life. As for me I thought I knew the solution to my life's problems and that solution was a man. I had no vision beyond today, because my life was revolved around him. Soon I became rebellious at home and my grades in school started dropping. The only thing I cared about was a man who would supply all my needs. Unfortunately, he was the reason why I lived. My life revolved around him. I would spend all of my time with him at his house and at school. We started ditching school together to be alone. I soon started falling for his lies and promises.

I will never forget a party that took place two years later. That night I ended up at his house and one thing led to another. I ended up giving him the most important gift the Lord had ever given me and that was my virginity. I refused to take a glimpse into tomorrow but focused on today. All I remember was thinking, *it's gone...why did I make this choice?*

At seventeen years of age, I became pregnant. I remember crying and telling him I didn't know what to do. I was still in school. I wasn't ready to be a mom...no way! I ended up making a decision that week that would change my life forever. I got an abortion. I remember waking up from my surgery thinking, *my goodness I killed my baby...what did I do?*

The guilt and the shame I was feeling only got worse. This man who told me he loved me and promised me a future, cheated on me. I was devastated. I started doing what anyone that is incomplete would do. I starting parting and smoking; yet those things could not complete me. I was so depressed that I even tried suicide a few times. I just didn't care about life anymore. Nobody, not even my parents, knew the internal scars, pain, anxiety, anger, hatred that I had to deal with.

I was so confused about life that I would go back with him even though he would cheat on me. I was so lost that I even ended up doing two weeks in jail. After eight years of hell, I finally found someone who loved me and cared about me. He gave me a vision of who I was and where I was going. This someone was Jesus. And life has been great since I hooked up with Him.

I want to encourage you to consecrate yourself everyday, read the word and pray. Fast once a week; believe me it works...stay focused! Don't give the enemy any chance to take what you got. If I would of known what I know now, believe me, I'd probably have a different testimony. But, thank God for His mercy that He has preserved me and allowed me to share with countless young ladies who have gone through what I went through.

I acknowledged my sin to unto thee, and my iniquity have I not hid. I said, I will confess my transgressions unto the LORD; and thou forgavest the iniquity of my sin.

Psalms. 32:5

God didn't have to forgive me, but He did. I will never forget what He has done for me. Every day I walk around declaring His promises. Some of you are probably saying, "I don't deserve to be loved by God because of all the things I've done." But let me remind you, "God came to seek and to save that which was lost."

Today, I am not living a life of pity or of shame but of praise and thankfulness. Although at times it is difficult for me to speak about my past and my pain. But you have to understand that the devil doesn't care. He is only out to kill and destroy us. He will do anything to destroy you! Instead of giving into sin, focus on what God has envisioned for you.

Pray for God to give you wisdom. Ask him for the courage to say "no" to sin. Ask Him for boldness. Have faith in God. He said He would supply all your needs. As you prepare to hear the word of GOD, ask him to give you a meek and teachable spirit. Let God do what he wants in you. Don't limit Him. Read a book or two, fast, pray, start a ministry, have a bible study or just simply tell somebody about Jesus. But, don't just sit around and waste time. For all of you who have gone through a situation similar to mine, don't feel discouraged or dismayed, but know that the Lord is on your side. He is willing and able to change your life, as He has done mine. And He is not done yet!

- Cecil is an inspiring young lady who has a powerful testimony. She is involved in Kings Daughters and a member of the AJC youth choir. She has a powerful praying ministry in which people have testified being healed.

REBECCA

Eight years ago part of my life left and didn't return. My father left our family. At that time I didn't know why dad didn't come home and why mom looked sad. As I grew in age I started understanding the real picture and that was they had gotten a divorce. My heart shattered into a thousand pieces and I remembered crying myself to sleep every night. It was during this trying time that I felt God holding me in His arms and reassuring me that He would never put more on me than I could bear. As the months turned into years there came times that I felt like giving up, it seemed Satan was whispering in my ear, "Your parents are divorced they will never get back together!" But I always ended where I started and that was with prayer. I was now in my teens and I feared not having a father figure. I knew the weaknesses, the failures, and the choices that girls with no father make. In my prayer, my parents coming back together were not an option it was a necessity. My future, my faith, my family was at stake. Eight years later from the time my parents divorced, the Lord performed a miracle in my life, that miracle was my father came back to us. My father and mother exchanged vows once again, that day was special not only because they got married again but it was also my sixteenth birthday. My parents are both serving God and active in our local church. This has been the greatest gift God could have ever given me – priceless! I realized through this lesson of brokenness that no matter what the situation is and how bad it presents itself, God can always turn it over for the good. Young people we need to be persistent with our prayer, praise Him no matter how impossible life or situations may look and know that God "is able to do exceeding abundantly above all that we ask or think, according to the power that worketh in us" (Ephesians 3:20).

- Rebecca is a member of the youth choir, active in youth ministry, and attends Morning Prayer faithfully. Her testimony has inspired and impacted numerous young people to "pray without ceasing"

What's your excuse?
What's your vision?
What's your story?

ENDNOTES

1. Frank Damazio, <u>Maximize Your Vision: Potential Seminar Syllabus</u> (Portland, 1990), 9.

2 Eastman Curtis, <u>Raising Heaven Bound Kids in a Hell Bent World </u>(Nashville, 2000), 62.

3. Curtis, <u>Raising Heaven Bound Kids in a Hell Bent World, </u>62.

4. Lane Palmer, <u>http://www.etamrevolution.net/quasar/is/content/ content.isi?channelid</u>

5. This is an anonymous story.

6. Warren Weirsbe, <u>The 20 Essential Qualities of an Authentic Christian</u> (Nashville, 1996), chapter 7.

7. <u>http://www.cyber-nation.com/victory/quotations/authors/ quotes_mulford_prentice.html</u>

8. Damazio, <u>Maximize Your Vision</u>, 37.

Printed in the United States
23411LVS00007B/139-306